R. Gupta's®

POPULAR MASTER GUIDE

Operation Theatre
Assistant

Recruitment Examination

Conducted by:

AIIMS, DSSSB, Haryana SSC, JIPMER,
PGIMER (Chandigarh) and Other Hospitals & Institutions

by
Pankaj Singhal
Graduate Nursing (AIIMS)

RAMESH PUBLISHING HOUSE, New Delhi

Published by
O.P. Gupta *for* Ramesh Publishing House

Admin. Office
12-H, New Daryaganj Road, Opp. Officers' Mess,
New Delhi-110002 ✆ 23261567, 23275224, 23275124

E-mail: info@rameshpublishinghouse.com
Website: www.rameshpublishinghouse.com

Showroom
● Balaji Market, Nai Sarak, Delhi-6 ✆ 23253720, 23282525
● 4457, Nai Sarak, Delhi-6, ✆ 23918938

Book Code: R-1763

ISBN: 978-93-5012-653-0

HSN Code: 49011010

Contents

OPERATION THEATRE ASSISTANT
Recruitment Exam

1. What is Analgesic drug?
   A. Drug which relief in pain
   B. Drug which increases heart rate
   C. Drug which decreases respiratory rate
   D. Drug reduces vomiting

2. What is Hypothermia?
   A. reduces temperature less than normal
   B. increases temperature more than normal
   C. increases heart rate
   D. decreases heart rate

3. Which is not a Regional Anaesthesia?
   A. Nerve blocks   B. General Anaesthesia
   C. Field blocks   D. None of them

4. Which is not a pre-operative checkup?
   A. Blood investigation
   B. MRI
   C. Ultrasonography
   D. None of them

5. What is the full form of ICU?
   A. Intra Cardiac Unit
   B. Recovery Room
   C. Intensive Care Unit
   D. Intra-operative Care

6. What is the colour of oxygen cylinder?
   A. White
   B. Black
   C. Body black and neck white
   D. Blue

7. What is the colour of N_2O (Nitrous oxide) cylinder?
   A. Blue   B. Black
   C. White   D. Yellow

8. What is the function of soda lime?
   A. Absorbs O_2 gas   B. Absorbs CO_2 gas
   C. Absorbs NO_2 gas   D. None of these

9. What length insert in the mouth of Endotracheal tube?
   A. 20-23 cm   B. 10-15 cm
   C. 40-45 cm   D. 5 cm

10. What is the formula of ET size calculation in children?

   A. $ID = \dfrac{age}{4} + 4\,mm$ B. $ID = \dfrac{age}{2} + 2\,mm$

   C. $ID = \dfrac{age}{3} + 4\,mm$ D. $ID = \dfrac{age}{4} + 2\,mm$

11. Which is not an Anaesthesia equipment?
   A. Anaesthesia machine
   B. CVP
   C. Pulse-oxymeter
   D. None of these

12. What is the function of sphygmomanometer?
   A. measures blood pressure
   B. measures pulse
   C. measures respiration
   D. None of these

13. Which function is not available in cardiac monitor?
   A. Pulse   B. Respiration
   C. Temperature   D. None of these

14. What is Normal Blood Pressure?
   A. 120/80 mm of Hg   B. 110/70 mm of H_2O
   C. 120/80 mm of H_2O D. None of these

15. What is the function of capnogram?
   A. measurement of expired CO_2 concentration
   B. measurement of inspired CO_2 concentration
   C. measurement of expired O_2 concentration
   D. measurement of Blood pressure

16. What is CVP?
   A. Central Venous Pressure
   B. Central Voluntary Pressure
   C. Central Vital Pressure
   D. None of these

17. What is normal CVP?
   A. 3-10 cm of H_2O B. 5-10 cm of H_2O
   C. 3-10 cm of Hg   D. 2-10 cm of Hg

18. What is ECG?
   A. Electro Cardio Gram

B. Electrical Cardial Gown
C. Electro Cardio Graph
D. None of these

19. What is EEG?
A. Electro Encephalo Gram
B. Electro Encephalo Graph
C. Electro Cardio Graph
D. None of these

20. Which is not Anaesthetic drugs gas?
A. O_2 B. N_2O
C. Ethylene   D. None of these

21. Which is not intra-venous drugs?
A. Proportal   B. Pentyl
C. N_2O D. None of these

22. *Rh* Factor related to:
A. Urine   B. Body excretion
C. Blood   D. None of these

23. How many blood groups are found in human body?
A. Two   B. Three
C. Four   D. One

24. What type of *Rh* factor is?
A. Rh (+) = 85%   B. Rh (−) = 15%
C. Rh^+ = 100%   D. 'A' and 'B'

25. Which is not a type of I.V. fluids?
A. Crystalloids   B. Colloids
C. Amino acid   D. Halothane

26. Which is not colloids?
A. Haemseal   B. Lomodex
C. Helastarch   D. None of these

27. What is cardiac shock?
A. Not properly working of heart muscles
B. Not properly working of lungs.
C. Not properly working of eye.
D. None of these

28. A patient going for spinal surgeries in operation, what position you will give him for surgergy?
A. Supine position
B. Prone position
C. Trendenburlg position
D. Knee-chest position

29. A patient going for Abdominal surgery, which position you will give in operation theatre?
A. Prone position

B. High follower position
C. Supine position
D. Lithotomy position

30. A patient (women) going for delivery with labour pain which position you will give?
A. Prone
B. Supine
C. Lithotomy
D. High follower position

31. What is Hypotension?
A. Decrease BP   B. Increase BP
C. Normal BP   D. None of these

32. What is Cryofreezing Anaesthesia?
A. Anaesthesia given by cryoprobe
B. Anaesthesia given by thermoprobe
C. Anaesthesia given by normal machine
D. None of these

33. Which is cryofreezing agent?
A. $CO_2 + N_2O$ B. H_2O + ice
C. Only ice   D. ice + N_2O

34. What is used for proportal?
A. Anaesthesia agent B. Antiemetic
C. Analgesic   D. Antipyretic

35. Which position is given in spinal Anesthesia?
A. Sitting Position   B. Lateral Position
C. Both A and B   D. None of them

36. What is sedatives?
A. Used for sleepness
B. Used for Anaesthesia
C. Used for depression
D. Both A and B

37. What is WHO?
A. World Health Organisation
B. World Happy Organisation
C. Wave Health Organisation
D. None of these

38. What is sterilization?
A. Process which killed all pathogenic organisms excluding spores.
B. Process which killed all pathogenic organisms including spores
C. Process which killed all pathogenic organisms not spores
D. None of these

39. What is pressure and temperature in Autoclave?

A. 121-132°C   B. 120-130°C
C. 110°C   D. 100°C

40. Which is chemical disinfection?
A. Glutaraldehyde   B. Fomaldehyde
C. Chlorine   D. Dry heat

41. Dry heat sterilization?
A. 170°C for 60 min.
B. 100°C for 50 min.
C. 120°C for 20 min.
D. None of these

42. What is universal precaution?
A. Precaution taken for HIV disease
B. Precaution taken for any disease
C. Precaution taken for any communicable disease
D. Both A and C

43. What is use of sponge count?
A. to prevent infection
B. long life
C. no need
D. None of them

44. Which drugs not needed in Resuscitation tray?
A. Adrenaline   B. Atropine
C. Normal Saline   D. None of these

45. What is occupational hazzards?
A. Fire
B. Chemical
C. Anaphylactic reactors
D. All the above

46. The following drugs should be discontinued prior to surgery
A. Prednisolone   B. Progesterone
C. Asprin   D. Propanolol

47. The following are intravenous induction anaesthetic agents.
A. Proportal   B. Halothane
C. Etomidate   D. Thiopentone

48. The following are significant advantages of regional anaesthesia?
A. Avoidance of unconsciousness
B. Absence of respiratory depression
C. Sympathetic blockade
D. Avoidance of Hypotension

49. Local Anaesthesia—
A. only affects sensory nerve fibres
B. is very effective for invasion and drainage

C. must be injected into the tissue to become effective
D. avoid convulsion

50. Complication of blood transfusion are:
A. Hypokalaemia   B. Hepatitis C
C. ARDS   D. Jaundice

51. What was the major objective of the Quit India Movement?
A. To gain complete independence
B. To win dominion status
C. To get more representation in the central legislative assembly
D. To ensure employment of more Indians in the Government

52. Article 51 of the Constitution of India lists
A. Fundamental Rights of Citizens
B. Duties of Citizens
C. Rights of Children
D. Human Rights

53. Who gave the slogan 'Back to the Vedas'?
A. Swami Vivekanand
B. Swami Dayanand
C. Raja Ram Mohan Rai
D. Sri Aurobindo

54. Which country is not a member of SAARC?
A. Nepal   B. Pakistan
C. Bhutan   D. China

55. An orange is a rich source of
A. Proteins   B. Carbohydrates
C. Vitamin C   D. Iodine

56. Which one of the following is the highest civilian award given to eminent persons?
A. Padma Vibhushan   B. Param Vir Chakra
C. Bharat Ratna   D. Maha Vir Chakra

57. Nagarjuna Sagar Dam is built across the river
A. Cauvery   B. Krishna
C. Narmada   D. Godavari

58. The film *'Guide'* was based on the novel of the same title written by
A. R.K. Narayan   B. Chetan Bhagat
C. Mulk Raj Anand   D. Jhumpa Lahiri

59. According to Mahatma Gandhi, what should be the medium of instruction at the primary stage?
A. Regional Language of the state
B. Hindi

C. English
D. Child's mother-tongue

60. Which one of the following is *not* a part of North-Eastern India?
A. Mizoram
B. Tripura
C. Andaman and Nicobar Islands
D. Nagaland

61. Which of the following is *not* a physical change?
A. Boiling of water to give water vapour
B. Melting of ice to give liquid water
C. Dissolution of salt in water
D. Combustion of Liquefied Petroleum Gas (LPG)

62. Which of the following gives the correct increasing order or acidic strength?
A. Water < Acetic acid < Hydrochloric acid
B. Water < Hydrochloric acid < Acetic acid
C. Acetic acid < Water < Hydrochloric acid
D. Hydrochloric acid < Water < Acetic acid

63. The ability of metals to be drawn into thin wires is known as
A. ductility
B. malleability
C. sonorosity
D. conductivity

64. Gunmetal contains
A. Cu = 60%, Sn = 40%
B. Cu = 80%, Sn = 20%
C. Cu = 70%, Sn = 30%
D. Cu = 90%, Sn = 10%

65. MRI stands for
A. Magnets Resonant Imaging
B. Magnetic Resonance Imaging
C. Magnetic Radar Imaging
D. Magnet Radial Imaging

66. What is the maximum resistance which can be made using five resistors each of $\frac{1}{5}\Omega$?
A. $\frac{1}{5}\Omega$
B. $10\ \Omega$
C. $5\ \Omega$
D. $1\ \Omega$

67. Which of the following is *not* associated with growth of plants?
A. Auxins
B. Gibberellins
C. Cytokinins
D. Abscisic acid

68. In a neuron, conversion of electrical signal to a chemical signal occurs at/in
A. cell body
B. axonal end
C. dendritic end
D. axon

69. Drinking alcohol is very harmful and it ruins the health. 'Drinking alcohol' stands for
A. drinking methyl alcohol
B. drinking ethyl alcohol
C. drinking propyl alcohol
D. drinking isopropyl alcohol

70. Which of the following elements does *not* lose an electron easily?
A. Mg
B. Na
C. K
D. Ca

ANSWERS

1	2	3	4	5	6	7	8	9	10
A	A	B	D	C	C	A	B	A	A
11	**12**	**13**	**14**	**15**	**16**	**17**	**18**	**19**	**20**
D	A	D	A	A	A	A	C	B	D
21	**22**	**23**	**24**	**25**	**26**	**27**	**28**	**29**	**30**
C	C	C	D	D	D	A	B	C	C
31	**32**	**33**	**34**	**35**	**36**	**37**	**38**	**39**	**40**
A	A	A	A	B	D	A	B	A	D
41	**42**	**43**	**44**	**45**	**46**	**47**	**48**	**49**	**50**
A	D	A	D	D	B	A	A	A	C
51	**52**	**53**	**54**	**55**	**56**	**57**	**58**	**59**	**60**
A	B	B	D	C	C	B	A	D	C
61	**62**	**63**	**64**	**65**	**66**	**67**	**68**	**69**	**70**
D	A	A	D	B	D	D	B	B	A

Chapter-1

PERIOPERATIVE PATIENT ENVIRONMENT

Introduction

Usually the treatment of a wide variety of illnesses and injuries include some type of surgical intervention. Surgery is an invasive method of treatment that may be planned or unplanned, major or minor, and that may involve any body part or system.

Surgical procedures require physical and psychosocial adaptations and are stressors for both the patient and the family, no matter what the extent might be. The patient's recovery from a surgical procedure requires skillful and knowledgeable nursing care whether the surgery is done on an outpatient basis or in the ideal operation room. All phases of the nursing process are used perioperatively to make assessments, arrive at a diagnosis, make appropriate plans and provide interventions necessary to:

- Promote the recovery of health,
- Prevent further injury or illness, and
- Facilitate coping with alterations in physical structure and function.

Three phases of the patient's perioperative experience:

(*i*) The preoperative phase,

(*ii*) The intraoperative phase, and

(*iii*) The postoperative phase.

Throughout the entire perioperative period

The assessment of patient needs is a continuous cycle which ensures that accurate and timely information for individualized patient care can be planned, implemented, and evaluated.

Home/Clinic/Holding Area

- Initiates preoperative assessment
- Plans teaching methods appropriate to patient's needs
- Involves family interview

Surgical Unit

- Completes preoperative assessment
- Coordinates patient teaching with other nursing staff
- Develops a plan of care

Surgical Suite

- Identifies patient
- Verifies surgical site
- Assesses patient's level of consciousness, skin integrity, mobility, emotional status, and functional limitations.
- Reviews chart

Surgical Unit

- Evaluates effectiveness of nursing care in the OR using patient outcome criteria
- Determines patient's level of satisfaction with care given during intraoperative period.
- Evaluates products used on patient in the OR.
- Determines patient's psychologic status.
- Assists with discharge planning.

Home/Clinic

- Seeks patient's perception of surgery in terms of the effects of anesthetic agents, impact on body image, immobilization
- Determines family's perceptions of surgery

Phases of the perioperative period

A. Preoperative phase—from the time the decision is made for surgical intervention to the transfer of the patient to the operating room.

B. Intraoperative phase—from the time the patient is received in the operating room until s/he is admitted to the recovery room.

C. Postoperative phase—from the time of admission to the recovery room to the follow-up home or clinic evaluation.

Organization of the Operating Room

Organization of areas in the operating room

The efficiency of the operating room depends much upon its physical organization and the organization of its personnel. An intelligent design in the layout of the operating room facilitates the efficient movement of patients and staff and the economical use of space.

Design of the Operating Room

Principles of Design

The universal problem of environmental control to prevent wound infection exerts a great influence on the design of the operating room (OR) suite. Clean and contaminated areas should be well differentiated. Architects follow two principles in planning the physical layout of the OR suite:

- Exclusion of contamination from outside the suite with sensible traffic patterns within the suite.
- Separation of clean areas from contaminated areas within the suite.

Physical planning of an OR suite, which separates clean from contaminated areas, makes it easier to carry out good aseptic techniques. The clean area is often referred to as the restricted area.

For operating rooms, there are many different designs. The basic design principles which are common to all operating rooms must fulfill the following criteria:

1. The design must always be simple and easy to keep it clean.
2. Wall and floor surfaces should be smooth and made of nonporous materials.
3. In order to prevent cross-contamination (the transfer of disease causing microorganisms from one source to another), there should be separate rooms for clean or sterile instruments and soiled ones.
4. There should be sufficient space to ensure the safe transportation of patients and staff.
5. The layout of the department should be convenient for the supervisor to control the incoming and outgoing traffics.
6. The recovery room should be near the operating room, so that patients can be transported safely and quickly following surgery.

Space Allocation within the Operation Room (OR) and Traffic Patterns

Space is allocated within the OR suite to provide for the work to be done, with consideration given to the efficiency with which it can be accomplished. The OR suite should be large enough to allow for correct technique, yet small enough to minimize the movement of patients, personnel, and supplies. Provision must be made for traffic control. The type of design will predetermine traffic patterns. All persons—staff, patients, and visitors—should follow the delineated patterns inappropriate attire. Signs should be posted that clearly indicate the attire and environmental controls required. The OR suite is divided into three areas that are designated by the physical activities performed in each area.

A. Unrestricted Area

- Street cloths are permitted.
- A corridor on the periphery accommodates traffic from outside, including patients.
- This area is isolated by doors from the main corridor and from other areas of OR suite.

- It serves as an outside-to-inside access area.
- Traffic, although not limited, is monitored at a central location.

B. Semi-restricted Area

- Traffic is limited to properly attired (dressed) personnel.
- Body and head coverings are required
- This area includes peripheral support areas and access corridors to the operating rooms.
- The patient may be transferred to a clean inside stretcher on entry to this area.
- The patient's hair must be covered

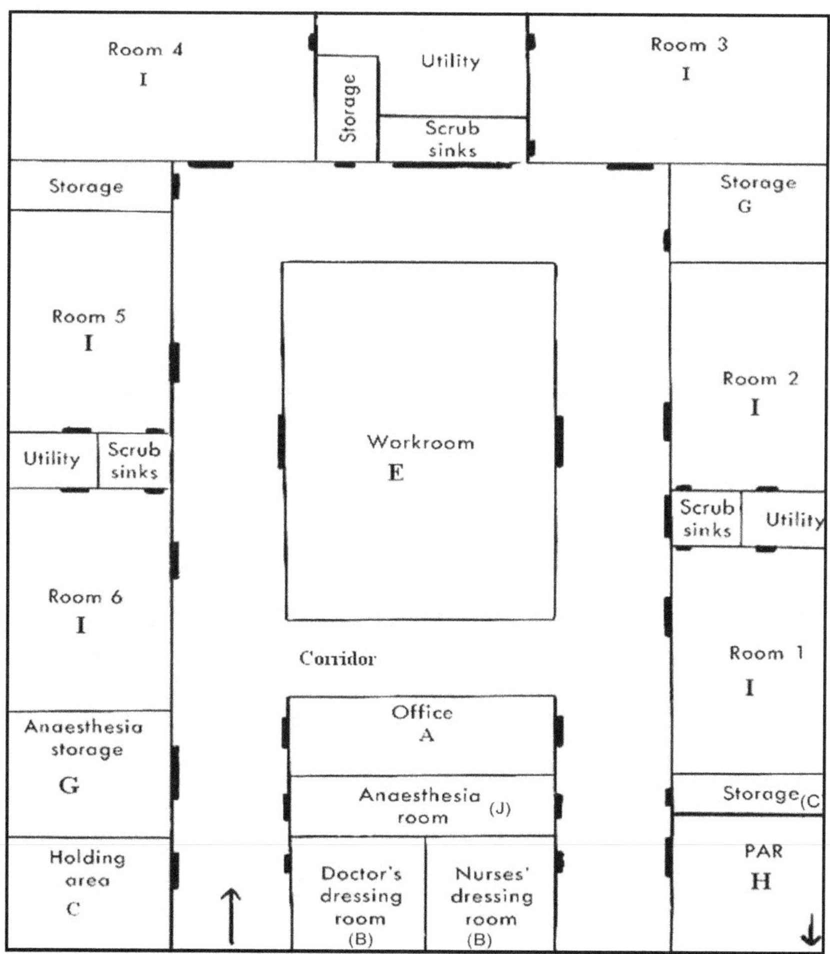

Fig. 1.

C. Restricted Area

- Masks are required to supplement surgical attire.
- Sterile procedures are carried out in this area.
- The area includes the operating rooms, scrub sink areas and substerile rooms or clean core area(s) where unwrapped supplies are sterilized.
- *The supervisor's office* (A) has direct access to the outside of the operating room. The supervisor may need to receive visitors and significant others who are not dressed in scrub attire.
- *Dressing rooms* (B) for operating room personnel has a door to the outside corridors so that personnel may enter there, change into scrub attire and go directly into the operating room.
- *The holding area* (C) is an area designated for the parking of stretchers with patients awaiting surgery. This is the area where the health care givers properly identify the patient and make sure that all preoperative cares are carried out and other important data are in the patient's chart.
- *Scrub sink areas* (D) are located in several places close to the operating suites. Scrub brushes, caps, soaps, masks are located at each scrub station.
- *The workroom* (E) is located so as to be away from the direct traffic of the operating suites. It is divided into two separate areas, one for clean instruments and supplies and one for soiled equipment.
- *The sterile supply room* (F) serves as a supply depot for wrapped sterile articles. This area should be dusted frequently with a damp cloth and have storage cabinets with doors to minimize exposure of the supplies to room air and dust.
- *Storage areas* (G) for extra equipment and supplies are used to store these extra instruments and supplies for each unit.
- *The recovery room* (H) has an access to the outside of the operating room for transporting patients back to their rooms.
- *The operating suites* (I) are rooms where surgery is performed. These rooms are wide enough to allows crub personnel to move around non-sterile equipment without their contamination.

Operating Room Equipment and Furniture

Wall Clock

Since time is often critical during surgery, each room should have a wall clock that is easy to read. The clock is used to time to urniquet applications, administration of medications, the duration of cardiac and respiratory arrests and to note the time of events such as childbirth.

X-ray Viewing Boxes

The surgeon may need to view an X-ray before or during the procedure.

Lights

The overhead lights should specially designed to provide arrange of intensity. They should be freely movable, shadowless and less heat emitting.

The Operating Table

The table should be fully adjustable in all directions to create postures needed for various surgical positions.

Mayo Stands

This stand is used to hold instruments that will be used frequently during a particular case.

Back Table

The back table is used to place extra supplies and instruments used during surgery.

Ring Stand

The ring stand is used to hold basins which contains norma saline or sterile water during surgery.

Kick Bucket

The kick bucket (a bucket on wheels) is used to place soiled sponges during surgery.

Supply Cabinets

These cabinets are used to store frequently used items such as drapes, dressings, solutions, sutures, etc. Cabinets with doors are preferred to those without so as to reduce exposure of the content to dust.

Anaesthesia Equipment

Equipment, including the gas machine, physiological monitor, anaesthesia supply cart, and sitting stools, is located in each room.

Operating Room Team

When the patient arrives to the operating room, he/she is received and surrounded by a surgeon, one or two assistants, an anaesthesia provider, a scrubbed nurse, a circulating nurse etc. These individuals, each with specific functions to perform, form the operating team. This team literally has the *patient's life in its hands*. The operating room team works in harmony with his/her colleagues for the successful accomplishment of the expected outcomes of the patient. The operating room team is sub-divided according to the functions of its members:

1. The sterile team consists of:
   (*a*) Surgeon
   (*b*) Assistants to the surgeon
   (*c*) Scrub nurse

2. The unsterile team includes:
   (*a*) Anaesthesia provider

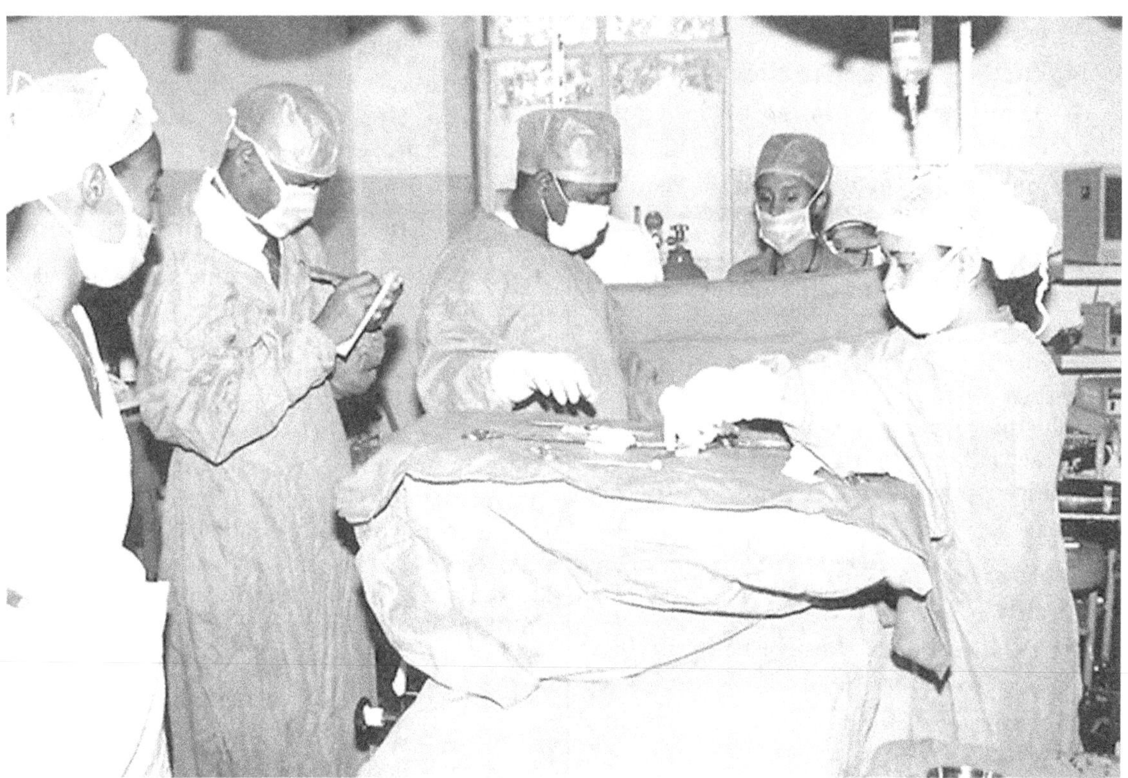

Fig. 2.

(*b*) Circulator/ Runner nurse

(*c*) Others, such as students, cleaners and those who maybe needed to set up and operate specialized equipment or monitoring devices

Responsibilities of the Anaesthesia Provider

Anaesthesia and surgery are two distinct, but inseparable disciplines; they are two parts of one entity. Adequate communication between the surgeon and the anaesthesia provider is the patient's greater safeguard. The anaesthesia provider is an indispensable member of the OR team. Functioning as a guardian of the patient, the anaesthesia provider should observe the principles of aseptic technique. The main activities of the anaesthesia provider are:

- Monitoring vital functions and parameters
- Fluid and electrolyte administration
- Administering anaesthetic agent/ anaesthesia
- Maintaining anaesthesia at the required levels
- Managing unto ward reactions to anaesthesia throughout the surgical procedure.

Medically delegated functions of an anaesthetic nature are performed under the overall supervision of a responsible physician or in accordance with individual written guidelines approved within the health care facility.

Responsibilities of the Assistant Surgeons

Under the direction of the operating surgeon, one or two assistants help to:

- maintain visibility of the surgical site
- control bleeding
- close wounds and apply dressings

Coordinated Roles of the Scrub Nurse and the Circulator

The Coordinated Role

- The circulator and the scrub nurses should plan their duties so that, through coordination of their efforts, the sterile and the unsterile parts of the surgical procedure move along simultaneously starts the surgical scrub until the surgical procedure is completed and dressings are applied, an invisible line separates the duties of the scrub nurse and the circulator, which neither person may cross.
- In the previous sections, the responsibilities of both the scrub and circulating nurses are listed separately, but a spirit of mutual cooperation is essential to move the schedule of surgical procedures efficiently and to serve the best interests of the patient.
- As a coordinated effort, the scrub nurse and the circulator nurse should complete the preparation of the environment.

Sponge, Sharp, and Instrument Count

Items are counted before and after use. The operating team members should be accountable for the performance of quality patient care. Accountability is a professional responsibility. The surgeon and patient rely on the accuracy of this accountability by the team. Item counts are performed for patient and personnel safety, infection control, and inventory purposes. An item left in the wound after closure is a possible cause for a lawsuit following a surgical procedure. A foreign body unintentionally left in a patient can be the source of wound infection or disruption.

Consequences of foreign body left in the patient's body will be:

- Formation of an abscess and development of fistula between organs

- Foreign body reaction may be immediate or delayed for years
- Sometimes difficult and costly to diagnose
- Removal of the object usually requires major surgery. A contaminated sponge or needle that is unaccounted for at the close of procedure could also in advertently come in contact with the personnel who clean the room. Blood or anyother body fluids are sources of pathogens such as Human Immuno deficiency Virus (HIV), Hepatitis B-Virus (HBV) or Hepatitis C-Virus (HCV). Inventory control is monitored by accounting for the instrument set in its entirety.

Counting Procedure

A counting procedure is a method of accounting for items put on the sterile table for use during the surgical procedure. Sponges, sharps, and instruments should be counted and/or accounted for on all surgical procedures. This includes any material introduced into the patient during the procedure. Acounting procedure is made three times in a surgical procedure.

A. First Count

The person who assembles and wraps items for sterilization will count them. In commercially prepackaged sterile items, the count is performed by the manufacturer.

B. Second Count

The scrub nurse and the circulator together count all items before the surgical procedure begins and during the surgical procedure as each additional package is opened and added to the sterile field. These initial counts provide the baseline for subsequent counts. Any item initially placed in the wound is recorded. A useful method for counting is as follows:

- As the scrub nurse touches each item, she/he and the circulator number each item aloud until all items are counted.
- The circulator immediately records the count for each type of item on the count record.
- Additional packages should be counted away from counted items already on the table, incase it is necessary to repeat the count or to discard an item. Counting should not be interrupted. The count should be repeated if there is uncertainty because of interruption, fumbling, or any other reason.

C. Third Count

Counts are taken in three areas before the surgeon starts the closure of a body cavity or a deep/large incision:

- **Field Count:** Either the surgeon or the assistant assists the scrub nurse with the surgical field count. Additional items are accounted for at this time.
- **Table Count:** The scrub nurse and the circulating nurse together count all items on the Mayo stand and instrument table. The surgeon and assistant may be closing the wound, while this count is in process.
- **Floor Count:** The circulating nurse counts sponges and any other items that have been recovered from the floor or passed off the sterile field to the kick buckets. These counts should be verified by the scrub nurse.

Qualities of the Operating Room Assistant

   (a) Stamina
   (b) Emotional stability
   (c) Stable health
   (d) Respect
   (e) Good Humour
   (f) Team spirit

Economical Use of Supplies and Hospital Equipment

Most of the hospital equipment is being imported from abroad and it is costly and, therefore economical and proper usage of it is mandatory.

As the cost of supplies and equipment increases, the OR team members should be conscious of ways to eliminate wasteful practices. For example, throw away disposable items only. Avoid throwing away reusable items.

The operation room is one of the most expensive departments of a hospital. Adequate instruments and supplies are necessary for patient care, and cost is not always the primary consideration. Economy becomes a hazard when exercised beyond the point of safety. Nevertheless, supplies do not need to be used lavishly, just because they are available. Remember the principles mentioned in the following sections.

"Just Enough is Enough"

The varieties and numbers of instruments and supplies needed for each surgical procedure can be kept to a minimum. Materials no longer used can be eliminated. Items to "have available" are not opened unnecessarily. The following procedures should be observed:

- Pour just enough antiseptic solution.
- Follow the procedures for draping.
- Do not open another packet of sutures for the last stitch unless absolutely necessary. A few leftover pieces are usually long enough to complete the closure.
- Supplies should be opened only as needed, not routinely "just in case" they may be needed.
- Turn off lights when they are not needed.

Chapter-2

INFECTION PREVENTION IN THE OPERATING ROOM

Infection Prevention

The infection prevention (IP) practices are intended for use in all types of health care facilities—from large urban hospitals to small rural clinics. The principles are based on the guidelines issued by Centers for Disease Control and Prevention, CDC (Atlanta, Georgia 1996).

The recommended infection prevention practices are based on the following principles:

- Consider every person potentially infectious and susceptible to infection.
- Washing hands before and after any procedure is the most practical procedure for preventing cross contamination.
- Donning (wearing) gloves before touching anything potentially infectious and wet such as broken skin, mucous membrane, body fluids, body secretions and excretions, or soiled instruments and other items—

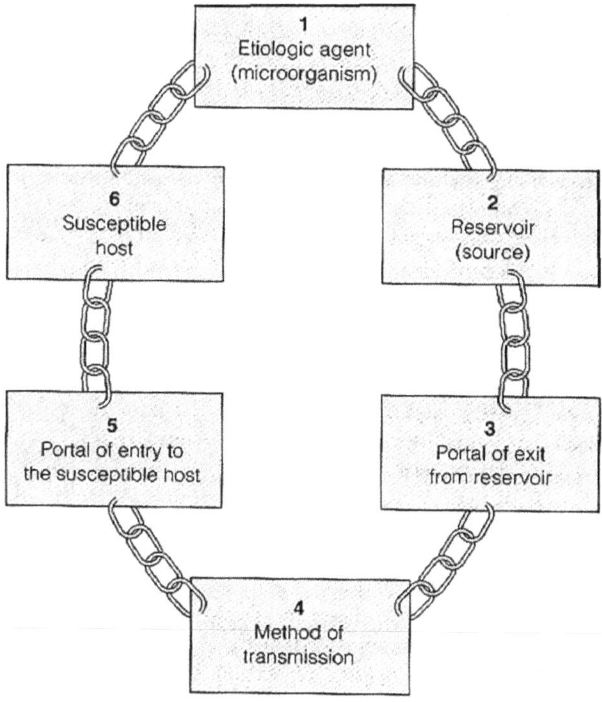

Fig. 1.

Hand Hygiene

Proper hand hygiene and the use of protective gloves in the operating room is a key component in minimizing the transmission of disease causing microorganisms and maintaining an infection-free environment.

Appropriate hand hygiene must be carried out:

- Before coming in direct contact with patients
- Before putting on sterile surgical gloves or examination gloves
- After any situation in which hands may be contaminated, such as (handling contaminated objects, including used instruments; touching mucous membranes, blood, body fluids, secretions or excretions except sweats)
- After removing gloves.

Hand Hygiene Techniques

Routine Handwashing

The purpose of handwashing is to mechanically remove soil and debris from skin and reduce the number of transient microorganisms. For appropriate handwashing:

- Thoroughly wet hands
- Apply a hand washing agent (plain soap or detergent)
- Vigorously rub all areas of hands and fingers for 10-15 seconds, paying close attention to fingernails, and areas between the fingers
- Rinse hands thoroughly with clean running water from a tap or a bucket
- Dry hands with personal dry clean towel, paper towel or air dry (using shared towel is not recommended as they quickly become contaminated).

Hand antisepsis

The purpose of hand antisepsis is to remove soil and debris and reduce both transient and resident flora on the hands. The technique for hand antisepsis is similar to handwashing except that it involves use of soap containing an antimicrobial agent instead of plain soap or detergent. Hand antiseptic should be done before:

- Examining or caring for highly susceptible patients (e.g., premature infants, elderly patients or those with advanced Acquired Immunodeficiency Syndrome (AIDS), etc.)
- Performing an invasive procedure such as placement of an intravascular device.
- Leaving the room of patients on Contact Precaution (e.g., Hepatitis A or E), or who have drug resistance infections.

Antiseptic Handrub

The purpose of antiseptic handrub is to inhibit or kill transient and resident flora. Use of a waterless, alcohol-based handrub product is more effective in killing transient and resident flora than antimicrobial handwashing agents or plain soap and water. Antiseptic handrub is quicker and easier to perform, and gives a greater initial reduction in hand flora.

This handrub solution contains a small amount of an emollient such as glycerin or sorbitol that protects and softens skin (Infection Prevention Guidelines, Federal Democratic Republic of Ethiopia Ministry of Health, Disease Prevention and Control Department, 2005).

A non-irritating, antiseptic handrub can be made by adding glycerin to alcohol (2 ml glycerin in 100 ml of 60% to 90% ethyl or isopropyl alcohol solution) *(Larson 1990; Pierce 1990)*.

Use 5 ml (about one teaspoonful) for each application and continue rubbing the solution over the hands until it is dry (15 to 30 seconds).

To be effective an adequate amount (5 ml) of antiseptic handrub solution should be used. For appropriate handrub:

- Apply enough alcohol-based antiseptic to cover the entire surface of hands and fingers.
- Rub the solutions vigorously into hands, especially between the fingers and under the nails until dry.
- Do not rinse hands after applying handrub. Alcohol based handrubs do not remove soil or organic materials, if hands are visibly soiled or contaminated with blood or body fluids, handwashing with soap and water should be done first. In addition, to reduce the "build up" of emollients on hands after repeated use of alcohol based handrubs, washing hands with soap and water every 5 to 10 applications is recommended *(Infection Prevention Guidelines 2005)*.

The term asepsis is used to describe the techniques of keeping the work area and personnel as free from microorganisms as possible with the intent of protecting the patient and the caregiver. The four important steps for the practitioner are:

1. Know what is clean, disinfected, or sterile.
2. Know what is not clean, disinfected, or sterile.
3. Keep clean, disinfected, and sterile items separate from contaminated items.
4. Take immediate action if contamination occurs. Practices and studies have showed that it is impossible to make the environment free from microorganisms. Although patient care situations and settings vary, basic principles of asepsis dictate the proper course of action to reduce microbial contamination. It is important that the basic principles of asepsis be consistently incorporated into patient care.

Infections in the health care settings may occur in the post-operative wound or as a complication unrelated to the surgical site. A post-operative infection is a very serious, potentially fatal complication that may result from a singlebreak in sterile technique. Therefore, the basis of prevention is the knowledge of causative agents and their controls as well as the principles of aseptic.

Sources of Contamination and Infection

1. Members of the operating team
2. The patients
3. All articles used in the wound and in the sterile setup
4. Dust in the air
5. Other personnel or visitor in the operating room.

The incidence and type of infections that occur in surgical patients may be the result of:

- A pre-existing localized infectious process,
- A systemic communicable disease, or
- An acquired preoperative complication

Need for Aseptic Technique

Strict aseptic technique is needed at all times in an operating room. Freshly cut living tissue can become infected easily. Therefore, it is essential for the nurse and all members of the operating team to know the common sources of microorganisms in an operating room and the means by which they reach the sterile field to contaminate it. The nurses must also know how to prevent contamination of a sterile field. Sterile technique is the responsibility of everyone in the operating room.

The principles of sterile technique are applicable, in various measures, to nursing in general. Their value will be demonstrated throughout the nursing care.

The Sterile Technique

Sterile technique is the basis of modern surgery. The patient is the center of the sterile field, which includes the personnel wearing sterile attire and the areas of the patient, operating bed, and furniture that are covered with sterile drapes. Strict adherence to the recommended practices of sterile technique reflects the surgical conscience of the perioperative team and is mandatory for the safety of the patient and personnel in the environment. The principles of sterile technique are applied under the following conditions:

- In preparation for an invasive procedure by sterilization of necessary materials and supplies.
- In preparation of the sterile team to handle sterile supplies and intimately contact the surgical site by scrubbing, gowning, and gloving.
- In the creation and maintenance of the sterile field, including skin preparation and draping of the patient.
- In the maintenance of asepsis throughout the surgical procedure.
- In terminal sterilization and disinfection at the conclusion of the surgical procedure. If these principles are understood, the need for their application becomes obvious.

Basic Rules of Asepsis

The outcome of a patient's surgical experience is influenced by the knowledge and application of aseptic technique by the peri-operative staff. All persons involved in the preparation and performance of surgical procedures are responsible for providing a safe environment for the patient. This is best achieved by maintaining asepsis and limiting the risk of contamination. To prevent infections, aseptic technique is practiced in the OR. This is implemented through the creation and maintenance of a sterile field. The center of the sterile field is the site of the surgical incision. In animate items in the sterile field include surgical items and equipment that have been sterilized by appropriate sterilization methods.

There are specific principles that the team members should understand to practice aseptic technique. Unless these principles are followed, the safety of the patient is compromised, and the potential for post-operative infection is increased. In addition to following the principles of aseptic techniques, the surgical team is responsible for following the guidelines established by the-occupational Safety and Health Administration (OSHA) and the Association of Peri Operative Registered Nurses to protect the patient and the team from exposure to blood borne pathogens.

Principles of Basic Aseptic Technique in the Operating Room

- All materials that enter the sterile field must be sterile.
- Sterile team members must wear only sterile gowns and gloves and they keep well within the sterile field.
- Unsterile persons don't reach over sterile surfaces.
- Talking during surgery is kept to a minimum.
- Bacteria travel on airborne particles and will enter the sterile field with excessive air movement and currents. Therefore, movement is kept to a minimum during surgery.
- Sterile team members face each other. They face the sterile field.
- Sterile personnel handle only sterile equipment.

- Unsterile personnel handle only unsterile equipment.
- If a sterile item comes in contact with an unsterile item, it is contaminated.
- If the sterility of an item is questionable, the item is considered as contaminated.
- Sterile tables are sterile only at table height.
- Gowns are sterile in front from the axillary line to the waist, and the sleeves to 2-3 inches above the elbow.
- The edges of anything that encloses sterile contents are considered unsterile.
- Moisture carries bacteria from a non-sterile surface to asterile surface.
- A wide margin of safety must be maintained between the sterile and unsterile field.
- Contaminated items should be removed immediately from the sterile field.
- The sterile field is created as close as possible to the time of use.
- Destruction of the integrity of microbial barriers results in contamination.
- Sterile persons keep contact with sterile areas/goods to a minimum.
- Some operative areas cannot be sterile. Steps are taken to keep contamination to a minimum.
- No compromise of sterility.

Standard Precautions

As established by the CDC and enforced by Occupational Safety and Health Administration (OSHA), standard recautions protect health care workers from contact with blood and body fluids of all patients. Standard precautions include considerations for the following:

- All body fluids
- Handwashing
- Barrier clothing
- Handling of used patient care equipment and linen
- Occupational exposure to blood-borne pathogens
- Patient placement.

Recommendations for standard precautions have been modified to reflect routes of transmission. The CDC-identified routes of transmission include, airborne, droplet, and contact precautions. The potential for becoming infected through skin exposure depends on:

- Localization
- Duration of contact
- The presence of skin lesions on the hands.
- Immune status of the host.

Standard precautions supplement other recommended practices for environmental control and are the minimum precautions for all invasive procedures. An invasive procedure involves any entry into body tissues or cavities in any procedural environment. Standard precautions are ineffect for any procedure during which bleeding occurs or for which the potential for bleeding or exposure to body-substances exists.

Application of Sterile Technique

Sterile technique prevents the transfer of microorganisms into body tissue during invasive procedures. Freshly incised or traumatized tissue can become infected easily, regardless of the area of the body. Intact skin and mucous membranes are the body's first line of defense against infection, but a portal for microorganisms is created if the integrity of the skin is interrupted.

Surgical procedures are performed under sterile conditions; contamination with microorganisms is prevented to maintain sterility throughout the procedure. A sterile field is created around the site of incision into tissues or the site of introduction of sterile instruments into a body orifice. Conversely, all material and equipment used during a surgical procedure are terminally decontaminated and sterilized after use with the assumption that every patient is a potential source of infection for other persons.

It is essential that all operating room team members know the common sources and mechanisms of contamination by microorganisms in the perioperative environment. Sterile technique is the particular responsibility of everyone caring for the patient in the OR. All members of the OR team must be vigilant in safeguarding the sterility of the sterile field. Any contamination must be remedied immediately.

Chapter-3

ATTIRE, SURGICAL SCRUB, GOWNING AND GLOVING

Historical Background

The evolution of special operating room **attire** as an adjunct to asepsis paralleled the development of **aseptic** and **sterile** techniques in the latter half of the nineteenth century. Many surgeons of that time continued to perform surgical procedures while wearing street clothes under pus- and blood encrusted aprons despite the expansion of germ theory knowledge.

One of the earliest mentions of specific OR attire appeared in a nurse's training handbook that advised the nurse to bathe before a surgical procedure, to take a carbolic bath before laparotomy, and to wear long sleeves and a clean apron for the surgical procedure. Long sleeves were recommended for anaesthesia providers and circulators to reduce the shedding of microorganisms and to protect them from contact with body substances.

The first use of caps and sterile gowns occurred in Germany, while principles of antiseptic surgery were still being debated *(Joseph Lister (1827–1912)*. In some ORs bacteria-laden, infection-causing woolen suits were replaced by OR garb made of sterilizable material that lessened the introduction of pathogenic microorganisms into the wound. The use of sterile gowns antedated the routine use of caps, gloves, and masks; although in 1883 **Gustav Neuber** (1850-1932) insisted that team members wear caps also.

Operating Room Attire

The techniques employed by operating room personnel when preparing themselves to take part in sterile procedures can be varied. However, the fundamental principles of aseptic technique must be adhered to when scrubbing, gowning and gloving prior to surgical intervention.

Purpose: The purpose of operating room attire is to provide effective barriers that prevent the dissemination of microorganisms to the patient and protect personnel from blood and body substances of patients.

Definition: Operating room attire consists of body covers, such as trousers, shirts, head covers, masks, gowns, gloves and shoe covers, as appropriate. Each has an appropriate purpose to combat sources of contamination external (exogenous) to the patient.

Dress code: The operating room should have specific written policies and procedures for proper attire to be worn within the operating room suite. The policies include:

- Dressing rooms are located in the unrestricted area of the OR suite.
- Only freshly laundered, clean attire is worn in the OR.
- OR attire should not be worn outside the operating room suite.
- Impeccable personal hygiene is emphasized (frequent and thorough handwashing, removal of jewelry,

keeping fingernails short and clean, denial of access to team members with acute infections ...).

- Comfortable, supportive shoes should be worn to minimize fatigue and for personal safety.
- Masks and head covers should be changed between patients.

Components of Attire: Body cover, head cover, shoe cover, mask, apron, gloves, gown, eyewear/goggles and face shield.

Criteria for Operating Room Attire: Attire should be:

- An effective barrier to microorganisms.
- Designed and composed to minimize microbial shedding.
- Made of closely woven material void of dangerous electrostatic properties.
- Resistant to blood, aqueous fluids and abrasion to prevent penetration by micro-organisms.
- Designed for maximal skin coverage.
- Hypoallergenic, cool, and comfortable.
- Made of a pliable material to permit freedom of movement.
- Able to transmit heat and water vapor to protect the wearer.
- Coloured to reduce glare under lights.

Surgical Scrub

The Surgical scrub is the process of removing as many microorganisms as possible from the hands and arms by mechanical washing and chemical antisepsis before participating in a surgical procedure. The surgical scrub is done just before gowning and gloving for each surgical procedure. Despite the mechanical action and the chemical antimicrobial component of the scrub process, skin is never rendered sterile.

Freeing the skin of as many organisms as possible, two processes are used:

Mechanical: This process removes soil and transient organisms with friction.

Chemical: This process reduces resident flora and inactivates microorganisms with an antimicrobial or antiseptic agent.

Purpose of Surgical Scrub

To remove soil, debris, natural skin oils, hand lotions and transient microorganisms from the hands and forearms of sterile team members. More specifically, the purposes are as follows:

- To decrease the number of resident microorganisms on skin to an irreducible minimum.
- To keep the population of micro-organisms minimal during the surgical procedure by suppression of growth.
- To reduce the hazard of microbial contamination of the surgical wound by skin flora.

Scrub Sink

- Adequate scrubbing and handwashing facilities should be provided for all operating team members.
- The scrub room is adjacent to the OR for safety and convenience.
- The sink should be deep and wide enough to prevent splash.
- Scrub sinks should be used only for scrubbing or handwashing.
- They should not be used to clean or rinse contaminated instruments or equipment.

Equipment

- Soft brush or disposable sponges
- Soap or detergent
- Running water.

Antimicrobial Scrub Agents

Various antimicrobial (antiseptic) detergents are used for the surgical scrub. The following are characteristics of the scrub agent:

- Broad-spectrum antimicrobial
- Fast acting and effective
- Nonirritating and nonsensitizing
- Prolonged action (*i.e.*, leaves an antimicrobial residue on the skin to temporarily prevent growth of microorganisms)
- Independent of cumulative action.

Although the action of the agent is important in relation to its efficacy, mechanical friction and effort while scrubbing are equally important.

Antiseptic and antimicrobial skin scrub products are chosen from among those approved by the Food and Drug Administration (FDA) for surgical hand scrub. Each product has a specific antimicrobial agent. Antiseptics alter the physical or chemical properties of the cell membrane of microorganisms, thus destroying or inhibiting cellular function.

The following is list of antimicrobial scrub agents:

- Chlorhexidine Gluconate
- Iodophors
- Triclosan
- Alcohol
- Hexachlorophene
- Parachlorometaxylenol.

Preparation for the Surgical Scrub

General Preparations

1. The skin and nails should be kept clean and in good condition.
2. Finger nails should not reach beyond the fingertip to avoid glove puncture polish can potentially crack and/or peel off as a result of which pathogens may be embedded underneath.
4. Artificial devices should not cover natural fingernails.
5. All Jewelry should be removed from the fingers and wrists (Because Jewelry harbors microorganisms).

Preparation Immediately Before the Scrub

1. Inspect the hands for cuts and abrasions. Skin integrity of the hands and forearms should be intact (without lesions and cracks).
2. Be sure all hair is covered by headgear including the ears.
3. Adjust the disposable mask snugly and comfortably over the nose and mouth.
4. Clean eyeglasses if worn. Adjust protective eyewear or the face shield comfortably in relation to the mask.
5. Adjust water to a comfortable temperature.

Surgical Scrub Procedure

The length of the surgical scrub varies depending on the following factors:

- The frequency of scrubbing
- The agent used and
- The method.

A vigorous 5-minute scrub with a reliable agent may be as effective as a 10-minute scrub done with less mechanical action. Prolonged scrubbing raises resident microbes from deep dermal layer so that they can be removed from the skin and therefore is more effective. Care should be taken not to abrade the skin during the scrub process. Denuded areas allow the entry of microorganisms.

Activities which bring individuals in contact with soil or other dirt need longer periods of scrubbing. For example, persons who participate in gardening, painting, mechanics etc. need longer time for scrubbing. Likewise, one who scrubs less frequently such as once every 3 to 4 days will need a longer scrub than a person who scrubs daily.

When gloves are removed at the end of the surgical procedure, the hands are contaminated and should be immediately washed. Resident microorganisms multiply rapidly in the warm, moist environment under the gloves.

Methods of Scrubbing

There are two methods of scrub procedures:

1. The counted brush-stroke method
2. The timed scrub method

If properly executed, they are both effective, and each exposes all surfaces of the hands and forearms to mechanical cleansing and chemical antisepsis. One should think of the fingers, hands, and arms as having four sides or surfaces.

In cases of a numbered stroke method, a certain number of brush strokes are designated for each finger, palm, back of hand, and arm.

The alternative method is the timed scrub, and each scrub should in average last 5-minute consisting of the following:

1. Locate scrub equipment (brushes, soaps, nail cleaners) which are available at each scrub station.
2. Remove Jewelry (watch and rings)
3. Wash hands and arms with soap and water
4. Clean subungual areas (with a nail)
5. Start timing - scrub each side of each finger, between the fingers, and the back and front of the hand for 2 minutes.
6. Proceed to scrub the arms, keeping the hand higher than the arm at all times. This prevents bacteria—laden soap and water from contaminating the hand)
7. Wash each side of the arm to 2 inches (5cm) above the elbow for 1 minute.
8. Repeat the process on the other hand and arm, keeping hands above elbows at all times. If at any time the hands touch any thing except the brush and or soap, the scrub must be lengthened by one minute for the area that has been contaminated.
9. Rinse hands and arms by passing them through the water in one direction only, from fingertips to elbow. Do not move the arm back and forth.

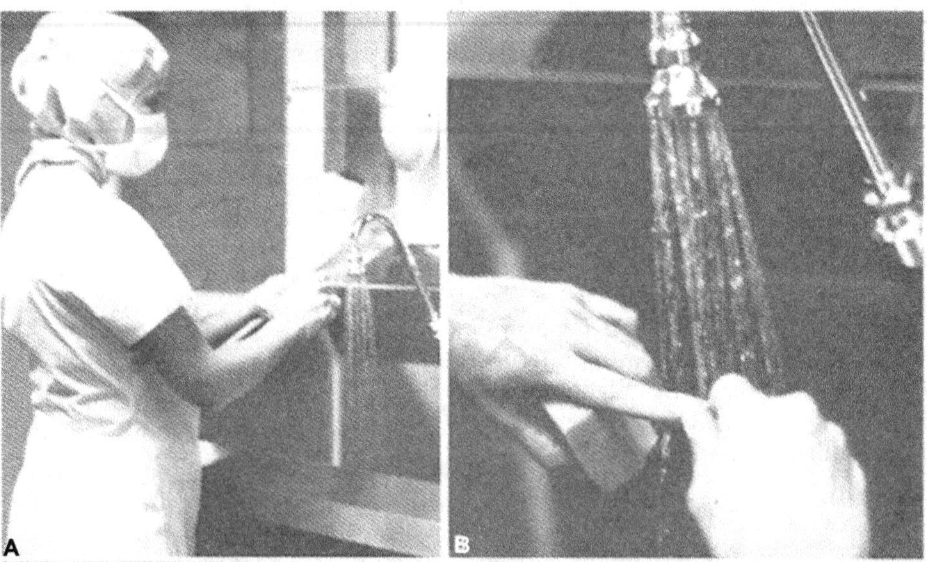

Fig. 1. *Technique for hand and arm scrub.* A. *Hands are washed as usual.*
B. *Subungual area is cleaned.*

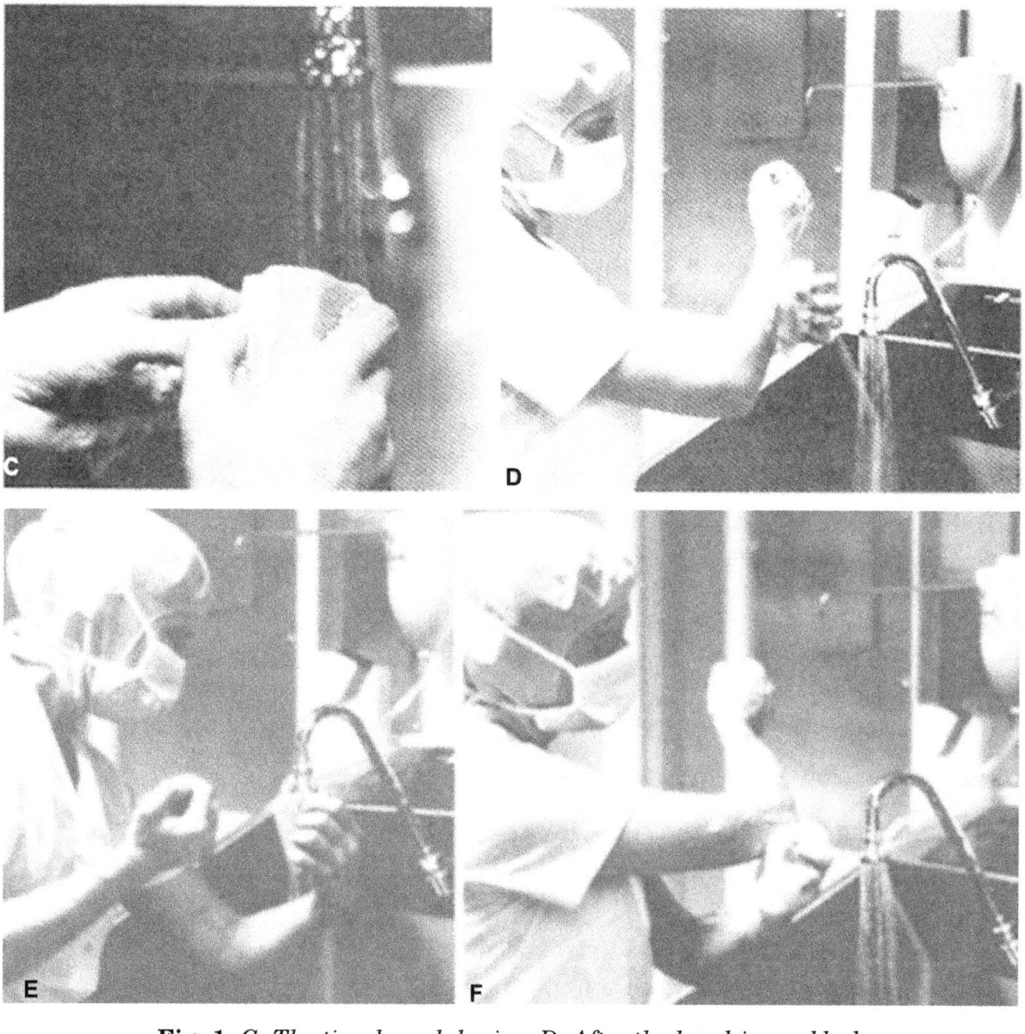

Fig. 1. *C. The timed scrub begins. D. After the hand is scrubbed, the arm is scrubbed and timed separately. E. The scrub extends to 3 inches above the elbow. F. The hand and arm are rinsed by passing them through the water in one direction only.*

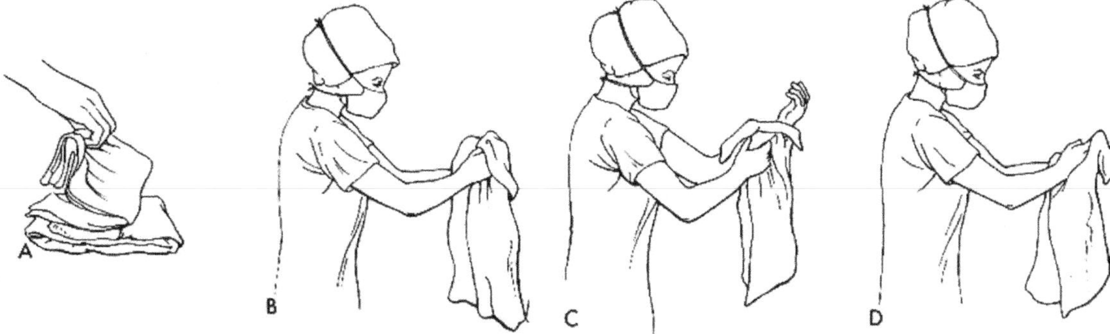

Fig. 2. *(A to F) Steps of drying the hands and arms*

Procedure of Drying Hands

1. Pick up a sterile towel from the open package put on the table, being careful not to drip water on the gown beneath it.
2. Use one end of the full-length opened towel only to dry one hand. Use a blotting motion as you dry.
3. Rotate the arm as you proceed to dry it, working from wrist to elbow. Do not allow the towel to contact the scrub.
4. Once the arm is dried, bring the dry hand to the opposite end of the towel and begin drying the other.
5. Dry the hand and arm using the blotting rotating motion.
6. Proceed to the elbow. Discard the towel into its proper place.

Gowning

- The purpose of wearing sterile gown is in order to provide sterile field
- There are two methods of sterile gowning:
  - Gowning self and
  - Gowning another.
- As the gown is donned:
  - The practitioners must ensure that they touch the inside of the gown only and that both arms are inserted into the sleeves of the gown together.
  - The circulating person should assist the scrubbed person by securing the gown's back ties. Scrub person, putting on gown, gently shake out folds, then slips arms into sleeves without touching sterile outside of gown with bare hands.

Circulator nurse, pulling gown on scrub person without touching the outside of the gown. Circulator nurse completes pulling on scrub person's gown, secures ties on inside of back, and closes fastener at neck.

Gloves and Gloving

This is the process of wearing gloves. Hand hygiene coupled with the use of protective gloves, is a key component in minimizing the spread of disease-producing microorganisms and maintaining an infection-free environment. In addition, understanding when sterile or high-level disinfected gloves are required and, equally important, when they are not, can reduce costs, while maintaining safety for both patient and caregiver.

Sterile gloves may be put on in two ways:

- By the closed gloving technique
- By the open gloving technique.

Types of gloves available in Ethiopia

- Sterile or high-level disinfected surgical gloves
- Clean examination gloves
- Utility gloves.

Wear gloves:

- When there is a reasonable chance of hands coming in contact with blood or other body fluids, mucous membranes or nonintact skin.
- Before performing invasive medical procedures (*e.g.*, inserting a urinary catheter).
- Before handling contaminated waste items or touch contaminated surfaces.

General Principles for Gloves Use

- All staff should wear appropriate gloves prior to contact with blood, body fluids, secretions or excretions from any client/patient.
- A separate pair of gloves must be used for each client/patient to avoid cross contamination.
- Wearing gloves does not replace the need for handwashing.

A. Closed Technique

1. Lay the glove palm down over the cuff of the gown. The fingers of the glove face toward you Fig. A.
2. Working through the gown sleeve, grasp the cuff of the glove and bring it over the open cuff of the sleeve.
3. Unroll the glove cuff so that it covers the sleeve cuff Fig. D and E.
4. Proceed with the opposite hand, using the same technique Fig. F, G, H and I.
5. Never allow the bare hand to contact the gown cuff edge or outside glove.

Closed technique self-gloving.

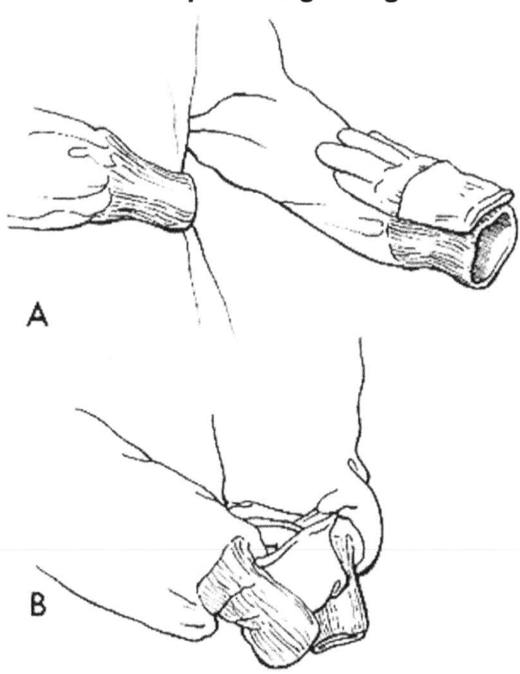

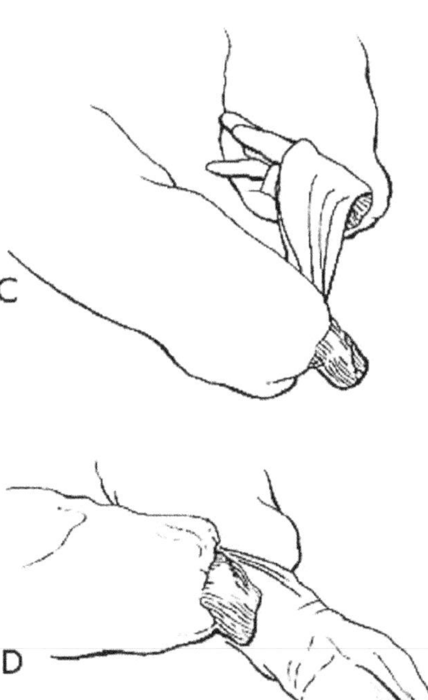

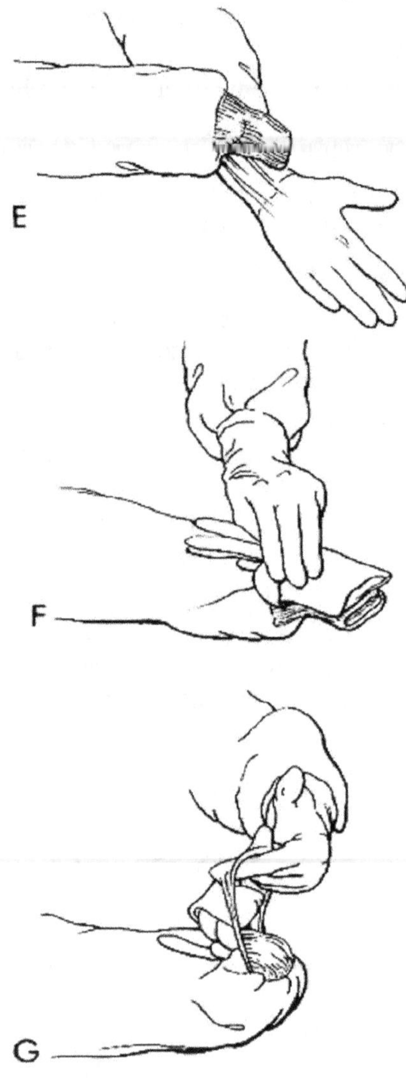

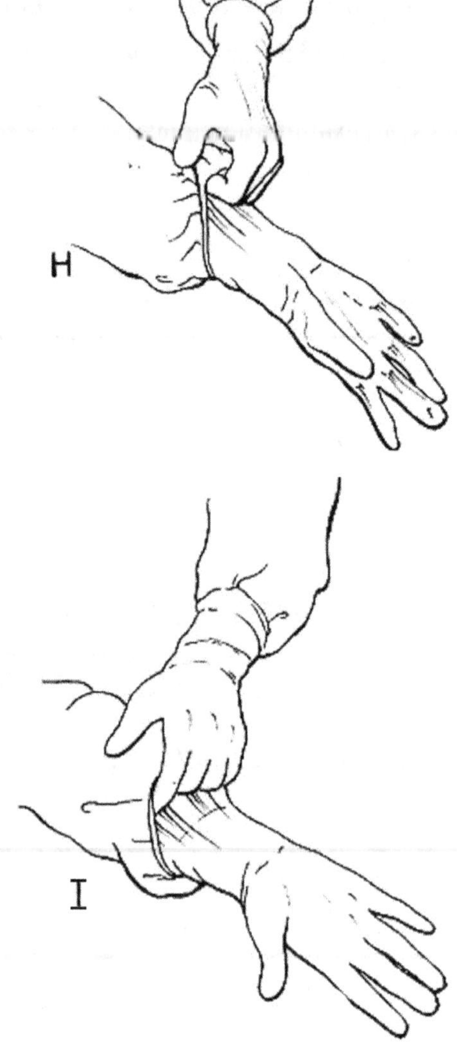

Fig. 3.

B. Open Technique

1. Pick up the glove by its inside cuff with one hand. Do not touch the glove wrapper with the bare hand.
2. Slide the glove onto the opposite hand. Leave the cuff down.
3. Using the practically gloved hand, slide the fingers into the outer side of the opposite glove cuff.
4. Slide the hand into the glove and unroll the cuff. Do not touch the bare arm as the cuff is unrolled.
5. With the gloved hand, slide the fingers under the outside edge of the opposite cuff and unroll it gently, using the same technique.

Techniques of Removing the Gown and Gloves

The gown is always removed before the gloves at the end of the surgical procedure.

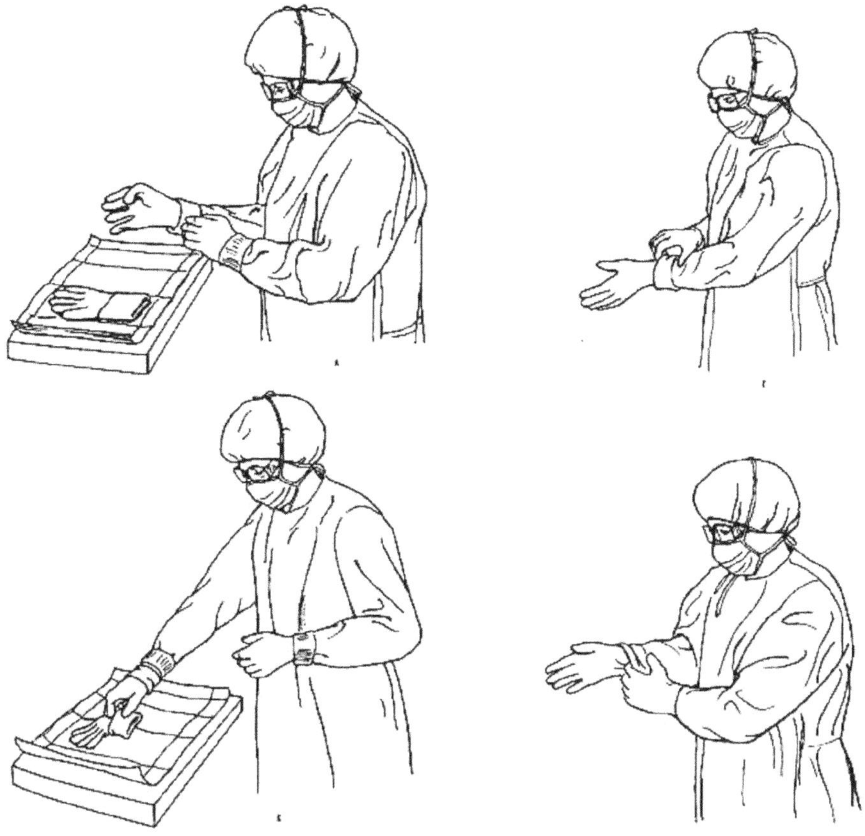

Fig. 4.

Removing the Gown

The gown is removed as follows:

1. Grasp the right shoulder of the loosened gown with the left hand and pull the gown downward from the shoulder and off the right arm turning the sleeves inside out.

2. Turn the outside of the gown away from the body with flexed elbows.

3. Grasp the left shoulder with the right hand and remove the gown entirely, pulling it off inside out (*See Fig.*).

4. Discard the gown in a laundry hamper or in a trash receptacle (if disposable). (A to C) sequence of scrub person removing soiled gown at the end of a surgical procedure. Clean arms and scrub suite are protected from contaminated outside of gown.

Removing the Gloves

The cuffs of the gloves usually turn down as the gown is pulled off the arms. A glove-to-glove, then skin-to-skin technique is used to protect the clean hands from the contaminated outside of the gloves. The gloves should be removed so that the bare skin does not come into contact with the outside of the soiled gloves.

Procedure

1. Grasp the cuff of the left glove with the gloved fingers of the right hand and pull it off inside out.

2. Slip the ungloved fingers of the left hand under the cuff of the right glove and slip it off inside out.

3. Discard the gloves in an appropriate receptacle.

4. Wash hands.

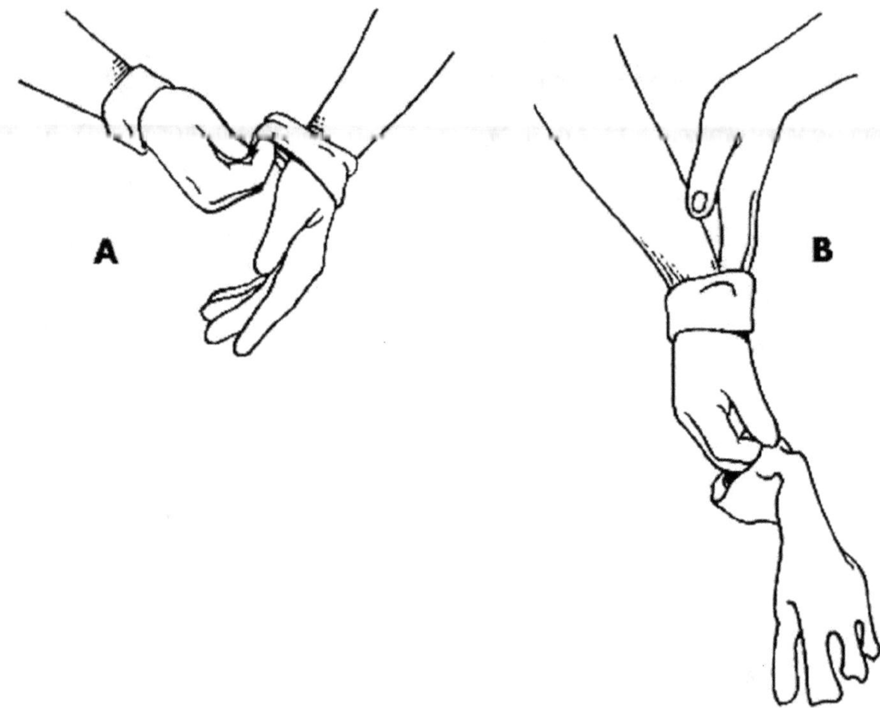

Fig. 5.

Methods of Distribution

Sterile items are packaged so as to allow personnel to unwrap the item without contaminating it. There are three popular methods of distribution.

A. Large linen packs

- Place in the center of the back table and unfolded using the prescribed technique.
- Pull layers towards the person opening the pack so that the hand and arm do not cross over the sterile area.
- Handle only the edge of the linen.
- Follow the same procedure for the final fold.

B. Small packages are opened by grasping the corners of the wrapper and bringing them back over the hand.

C. A third method of distribution is the peel-back wrapper/package. Supplies are contained within the package, which is peeled apart to expose the sterile item). Solutions such as sterile saline or water are poured into basins carefully so as to avoid splash.

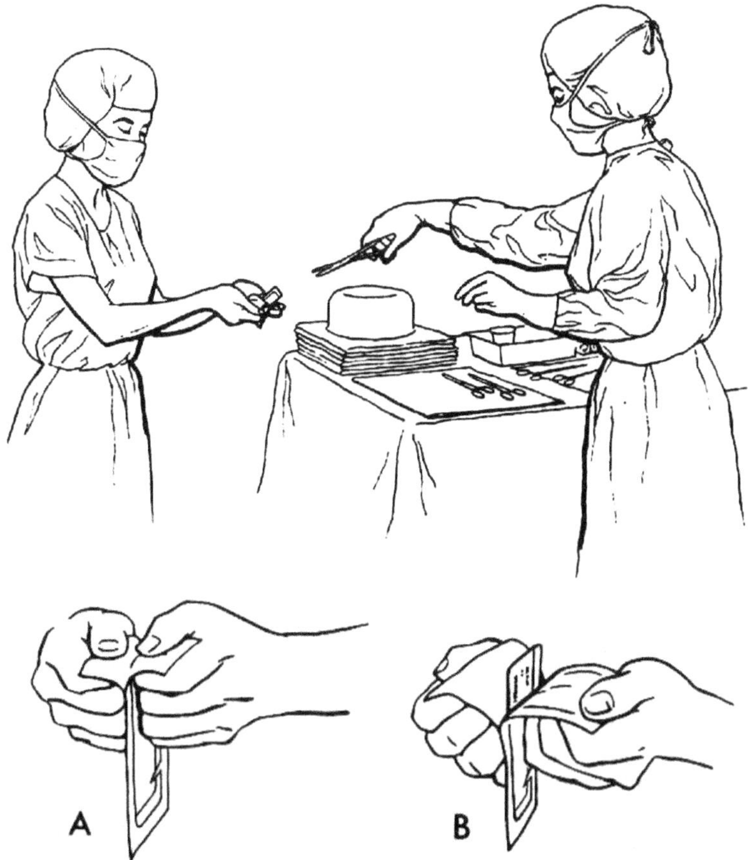

Fig. 6. *Scrub person taking contents from suture packet opened and held by circulator. Scrub person avoids touching unsterile outer wrapper.*

Cleaning the operating room and instruments

Cleaning is the process that physically removes all visible dust, soil, blood or other body fluids from inanimate objects including the OR floor and walls to reduce risks of disease transmission in the OR. Cleaning can be made in daily (at the beginning of the day's activity, in between the cases, and at the end of the day) as well as on weekly basis. Areas to be considered are walls, floors, ceilings, storage shelves, all furniture and equipment in the OR including the operating bed/table. Following a surgical case, after the patient has left the OR, the nurse gathers all of the instruments (including soiled and terminal decontamination).

1. All linen is placed in the linen hamper.
2. Disposable items in the trash.
3. Large equipment is wiped with a disinfectant and placed in its usual storage.
4. The floors are cleaned with disinfectant.
5. The stationary equipment (operating table, electrosurgical power unit, etc) are all wiped clean with disinfectant.
6. Any visible soil is washed with disinfectant.

Chapter-4

STERILIZATION

Introduction

Procedures for sterilizing equipment and supplies are based largely on principles of microbiology. There are two common methods by which items can be sterilized (physical and chemical).

Sterilization is the process by which all pathogenic and nonpathogenic microorganisms, including spores, are killed. It is the only process that ensures that an item is free from all microbes. Sterilization can be achieved with physical or chemical methods. Physical methods generally rely on moisture dry heat. Chemical methods on the other hand, use gaseous or liquid chemicals.

Methods of Sterilization

Chemical Methods

Ethylene oxide (EO or ETO) gas is used to sterilize items that are sensitive to heat or moisture. EO must have direct contact with microorganisms on or in the items to be sterilized. EO is highly flammable and explosive in air and therefore, must be used in an explosion-proof sterilizing chamber in a controlled environment. When handled properly, EO is reliable and safe for sterilization, but the toxic emission and residues of EO present health hazards to healthcare providers and patients. Its effectiveness depends on four parameters which include:

- Concentration of EO gas
- Temperature
- Humidity
- Time (duration of gas exposure).

Glutaraldehyde 2% and formaldehyde 8% can also be used as a chemical sterilizer (refer see fig.).

Physical Methods

Heat is a dependable physical agent for the destruction of all forms of microbial life, including spores. It may be used moisture dry. The most reliable and commonly used method of sterilization is steam under pressure.

A. Moist heat (steam under pressure) or autoclave

This method is the least expensive, most efficient, and least time-consuming method and is the method of first choice, whenever possible. For the steam process to achieve sterility, the time, temperature, pressure, and moisture must be present in correct proportions. An imbalance in these components can result in failure of the process. The minimum time for the entire cycle in the autoclave sterilizer is 25 to 30 minutes at 121 to 132 degrees celsius. However, it is possible, but not recommended to speed up the process in the autoclave sterilizer by:

- Increasing the temperature
- Decreasing the time
- Processing the item unwrapped.

This method is called **flash/high-speed pressure** sterilization. Because the delicate

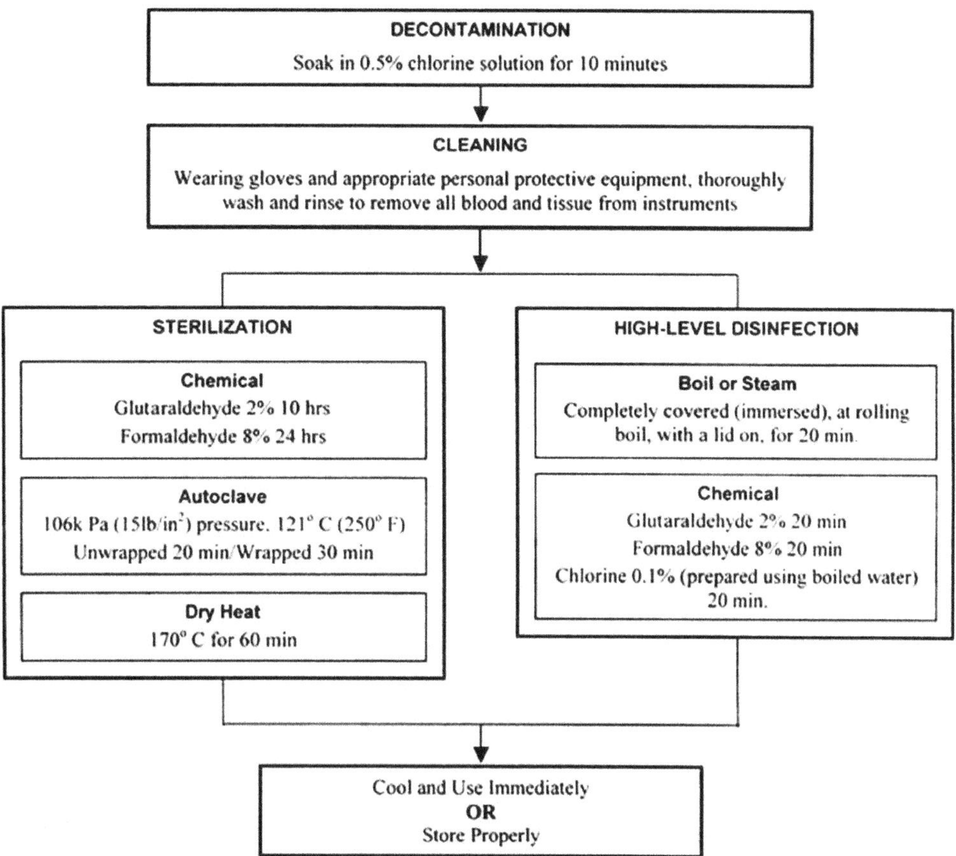

Fig. 1. *Key Steps in Processing Contaminated Items*

balance among processing time, temperature, pressure, and moisture are changed, the probability that sterility will be achieved is reduced.

For this reason, flash sterilization should be used only in an emergency (*e.g.*, a surgical instrument has been dropped, no alternative exists, and the instrument is needed immediately).

Advantages of Steam Sterilization

- It is the easiest, safest and surest method of on-site sterilization.

- Steam is the fastest method; its total time cycle is the shortest.

- Steam is the least expensive and most easily supplied agent.

- Most sterilizers have automatic controls and recording devices that eliminate the human factor from the sterilization process.

- Steam leaves no harmful residue. Many items such as stainless steel instruments withstand repeated processing without damage.

Disadvantages of Steam Sterilization

- Precautions must be used in preparing and packaging items, loading and operating the sterilizer, and drying the load.

- Items need to be clean, free of grease and oil, and not sensitive to heat.

- Steam must have direct contact with all areas of an item. It must be able to penetrate packaging material, but the material must be able to maintain sterility.

- The timing of the cycle is adjusted for differences in materials and sizes of loads; these variables are subject to human error.

B. Dry Heat

By this method, the items to be sterilized are subjected to heated air in an enclosed oven or container. This method is usually reserved for sterilizing powders, oils, sharps, sponges, and bandages. The major disadvantages of dry heat are that it penetrates materials slowly and unevenly.

Sterility Indicators and Control Monitors

It is necessary to have a reliable, inexpensive method for checking the effectiveness of a sterilizing process.

- Packages wrapped for sterilization are sealed with indicator tape.

- Tape used on packs to be steam sterilized has temperature sensitive areas that change colour when exposed to high temperatures.

- Tape used on packs to be gas sterilized has areas that change colour upon exposure to the used (EO). Other indicators, in the form of paper strips or gas vials, are also available for insertion within the package. These indicators are called process monitors. It is important to note that these indicators reveal only that the pack has undergone a sterilization process. It does not indicate that the item is sterile. The most efficient method of testing sterility is with biological controls.

- A highly resistant, non-pathogenic, spore-forming bacteria, contained in a glass vial or impregnated onto a strip of paper, is placed in the load to be sterilized.

- For steam sterilization, the dry spores of the bacteria *Bacillus stearothermophilus* are used; gas sterilization uses *Bacillus subtilis*.

- The vial or strip is recovered at the end of the sterilization process and cultured. This process is time-consuming and the results may not be known for several days, but it is a very reliable method of testing the efficacy of a sterilization process.

Shelf Life

The length of time an item can be considered sterile is referred to as the **shelf life**.

Sterility is event related; it is not time related unless the package contains unstable components such as drugs or chemicals. Storage conditions are established to maintain the integrity of the package. An item is considered sterile on the basis of the following events:

- Handling of the package during transport and storage (*i.e.*, the prevention of contamination and physical damage).

- Integrity, type, and configuration of packaging material.

- Condition of storage.

Most commercially sterilized products are considered sterile indefinitely or as long as the integrity of the package is maintained. An expiration date put on the label by the manufacturer indicates the maximum time the manufacturer can guarantee product stability and sterility on the basis of test data approved by the FDA.

Integrity of Packaging Material and Handling

The method of sterilization establishes the type of packaging material that may be used. Shelf life is affected by the:

- Permeability and density of the material

- Type of closure used

- Method by which the package is handled.

The following are considerations regarding the integrity of packaging materials:

- An item is no longer considered as sterile after an accidental puncture, tear, or rupture of the package.

- Squeezing or crushing a package may force air out and draw unsterile air in, thus contaminating the contents.

- The accidental wetting of a package contaminates the contents.

It is necessary to avoid the following:

- Handling the package with moist or wet hands

- Handling the package with soiled gloves

- Placing the package on a wet surface

- Commercially packaged, sterilized items are usually considered sterile until the package is opened or damaged or the stability of the product becomes outdated.

Dust Cover

A sealed, airtight plastic bag protects a sterile package from dust, dirt, lint, moisture, and vermin during storage. After sterilization and immediately following aerating or cooling to room temperature, infrequently used items may be sealed in plastic 2 to 3 mil thick. A dust cover will protect the integrity of the package.

Storage Conditions

The maintenance of sterility is related to the event and is not based on time. How sterile packages are handled and stored is as important as how long they can remain sterile. The following guidelines are helpful in maintaining the sterility of a package during storage:

- Storage areas are clean and free of dust, lint, dirt, and vermin. Routine cleaning procedures are followed for all areas in the peri-operative environment.

- All sterile items should be stored under conditions that protect them from the extremes of temperature and humidity.

Chapter-5

DISINFECTION

Introduction

Terminal decontamination, disinfection, and sterilization are the procedures carried out for the destruction of pathogens on items at the end of use for patient care during a surgical procedure. Methods and procedures for disinfection vary according to the intended use of the disinfected item. Personal protective equipment should be worn while using chemical disinfecting agents. Disinfection eliminates pathogenic microorganisms on inanimate objects, with the exception of bacterial spores. This is generally achieved in health care settings by the use of liquid chemicals or boiling.

Factors that influence the effectiveness of Disinfectant

These include the following:

A. **Nature of the item:** The crevices, joints, and hinges, the more difficult it is to disinfect.

B. **Number and type of micro-organisms present on the object:** The higher the level of the item's contamination, the difficult it is to disinfect. Some microbes are more difficult to kill than others.

C. **Amount of soil or organic matter present:** Soil protects microbes and may inactivate the disinfectant solution.

D. **Contact time:** Disinfection requires direct contact with the agent for a specific time.

E. **Concentration of solution:** The more concentrated the solution has, the greater is its killing capacity. The solution must be used at the concentration specified by the manufacturer to be most effective.

This system was adopted and later modified by the Centers of Disease Control and Prevention (CDC).

A. **Critical items** must be sterile because they enter sterile tissue, break the mucosal barrier, or come into contact with the vascular system. Examples include surgical instruments, catheters, needles, implants etc.

B. **Semi-critical** items come into contact with non-intact skin and mucous membranes and require high-level disinfectional though they may also be sterilized. Examples include respiratory therapy equipment, anaesthesia equipment, bronchoscopes, colono-scopies, gastroscopes, sigmoidoscopes, and cystoscopes.

C. **Non-critical** items are used in contact only with intact skin. Intermediate or low-level disinfection is adequate. Examples include blood pressure cuffs, furniture, linens, bedpans.

Levels of Disinfection

Disinfectants vary in their ability to kill microorganisms. The levels of disinfection described are low, intermediate, and high. High-level disinfectants are effective against:

- All vegetative bacteria
- Viruses
- Fungi
- Tuberculosis (TB).

Most high level disinfectants have a demonstrated level of activity against bacterial spores. High-level disinfectants are used primarily for such semicritical items as:

- Laryngoscopes
- Respiratory therapy and anaesthesia equipment
- Flexible fibroptic endoscopes.

Intermediate-level disinfectants are more powerful and kill more resistant microorganisms than low-level disinfectants. In addition to vegetative bacteria, fungi, and lipid-involved viruses, they are effective against *Mycobacterium tuberculosis* and nonlipid viruses. They are not effective against resistant bacterial spores. Chlorine, iodophors, phenolics, and alcohol belong to this group. Low-level disinfectants kill most vegetative bacteria, fungi, and lipid-enveloped viruses, but do not ill spores or nonlipid viruses. They are less active against the *Mycobacterium tuberculosis* and some gram-negative rods, such as pseudomonas. These disinfectants are typically used to wipe down items that will contact only intact skin or for environmental surface disinfection.

Methods of Disinfection

Many products and methods are used to disinfect instruments. A few are described below:

Chemical Disinfectants

Formaldehyde (37% aqueous; 8% alcohol)

- Kills microorganisms by coagulating protein in the cells
- The solution is effective at room temperature
- It has a pungent odor and is irritating to the eyes and nasal passages

- Its vapours can be toxic.

Hydrogen Peroxide—interacts with cell membranes, enzymes, or nucleic acids to disrupt the life functions of microorganisms.

Alcohol—Ethyl or isopropyl, 70% to 95%, kills microorganisms by coagulation of cell proteins.

Chlorine Compounds—kill microorganisms by the oxidation of enzymes.

Glutaraldehyde—kills microorganisms by denaturation of protein. It is most commonly used in a 2% solution.

Iodophore—a complex of free iodine with detergent, kills microorganisms through a process of oxidation of essential enzymes.

Physical Disinfectants

Boiling/pasteurization— is a method of thermal disinfection that involves immersion of pre-cleaned items into water heated to approximately 75° to 100°C for 30 min.

Boiling method:

- Cannot be depended on to kill spores
- Is a nontoxic, high-level disinfection process.

Guidelines for Boiling

1. Never put fecally contaminated instruments in the boiler.
2. Instruments to be boiled should totally be submerged.
3. Timing should be counted when the water comes to its full boil.
4. Change the water in the boiler every day or every two days since as the water boils it leaves a scum of impurities which will stain the inside of the boiler and spoil the instrument.
5. Boil instruments separately.
6. Inspect the boiler from time to time and keep it in good condition.
7. Do necessary repairs before anything goes really wrong.

Disinfectant	Activity Level	Virucide		Immersion Time	Housekeeping	Hazards
		HIV	HBV	Tuberculocide		
Chemicals*						
Alcohol, 70%-95%						
Ethyl	Intermediate	Yes	Yes	15 minutes	Yes	Flammable
Isopropyl	Intermediate	Yes	No	15 minutes	Yes	Flammable
Chloride compounds	Low	Yes	Yes	N/A	Yes	
Formaldehyde						
37% aqueous	High	Yes	Yes	15 minutes	No	Toxic fumes
8% in alcohol	High	Yes	Yes	10 minutes	No	Toxic fumes
Glutaraldehyde, 2%	High	Yes	Yes	45-90 minutes	No	Irritating fumes
Iodophors						
450 ppm	Intermediate	Yes	Yes	20 minutes	Yes	
100 ppm	Low	No	No	N/A	Yes	
Mercurial compounds	None	No	No	N/A	No	Bacteriostatic only
Phenolic compounds	Low	Yes	No	20 minutes	Yes	Skin irritant
Quaternary ammonium	Low	Yes	No	N/A	No	
Physical						
Boiling water	Low	Yes	No	N/A	No	
Ultraviolet irradiation	Low	Yes	No	N/A	Air and water	Skin and eye irritant

Care of Instruments

Surgical instruments are expensive and represent a major investment. Surgical procedures have become more complicated and intricate and, as a result, instruments have become more complex, more precise in design, and more delicate in structure. Abuse, misuse, inadequate cleaning or processing, or rough handling can damage and reduce the life expectancy of even the most durable instrument, and the cost of repair or replacement becomes unnecessarily high. Instruments can last for many years if they are handled or maintained properly. Careless handlings of the surgeon's tools (instruments) results in frustration for the surgeon and great financial loss to the department or hospital.

The skills of the surgeon are hampered if he/she is forced to work with inferior equipment such as:

- Scissors that are dull.
- Clamps that won't stay closed over bleeding vessels.
- Needle holders that pop open to release the needle into the wound.
- Forceps whose teeth don't mesh (fit) together properly.

It is the nurse's responsibility to care for the proper handling and maintenance of the instruments.

Guidelines which help increase the lifespan of instruments and ensure their proper function include:

During surgery

- Handle instruments gently.
- Don't throw them into basins.
- Keep the sharp surfaces of cutting instruments away from other metal surfaces that could dull them.
- Don't soak them in saline solution
- When feasible, wipe blood to cake and dry on the instrument.
- Use the correct instrument for the job at hand.
- Heavy needles will damage delicate needle holders.
- Wire sutures must be cut with wire cutters, not suture scissors.
- Use towel clips and not hemostats for securing drapes.

After surgery

- Decontaminate/clean instruments as soon as possible. Don't allow blood to dry on them.
- Use accepted techniques when sterilizing instruments.
- Separate sharp or delicate instruments from others when processing.
- Process all instruments from a surgical case, whether or not they have been used.

NB. Lubrication of instruments before they are wrapped is important. Lubrication in water soluble antimicrobial solution prevents hinges and box locks from becoming stiff and protects sharp surfaces of the metal.

Decontaminating and Cleaning of Instruments

Decontamination is the first step in handling used instruments and supplies. Immediately after use, all instruments should be placed in an approved disinfectant such as 0.5% chlorine solution for 10 minutes to inactivate most organisms, including HBV and HIV (ARON 1990; ASHCSP 1986). It is a process that makes inanimate objects **safer** to be handled by staff **before** cleaning. Decontamination is performed in a designated area, not in the OR, immediately after completion of the surgical procedure.

For achieving satisfactory decontamination:

- Make fresh solution every morning, or more often if the solution becomes cloudy.
- Use plastic, non-corrosive container for decontamination. This prevents sharp instruments from getting:

  - Dull due to contact with metal containers.
  - Rusted due to chemical reaction that can occur between two different metals when placed in water.

- **Do not** soak metal instruments in water for more than one hour, even if they are electroplated, to preven trusting
- **Do not** mix chlorine solutions with either formaldehyde or with water

Formula for Making a Dilute Solution from Concentrated Solutions

- Determine the concentration (% concentration) of the chlorine solution.
- Determine the desired concentration % dilution.
- Check concentration (% concentrate) of the chlorine product you are using.
- Determine total parts water needed using the following formula:

Total Parts (TP) water

$$= \left[\frac{\% \text{ Concentrate}}{\% \text{ Dilute}} \right] - 1$$

- Mix 1 part concentrated bleach with the total parts water required.

Example: Make a dilute solution (0.5%) from 5% concentrated solution.

STEP 1: Calculate TP water:

$$\left[\frac{5.0\%}{0.5\%} \right] - 1 = 10 - 1 = 9$$

STEP 2: Take 1 part concentrated solution and add to 9 parts water.

Effectiveness of Methods for Processing Instruments.

Method	Effectiveness	End point
Decontamination	(Kill or remove microorganisms) Kills HBV and HIV and most microorganisms	10 minute soak
Cleaning	(Water and soap only)	Up to 80% until visibly clean Up to 50% until visibly clean
High-Level	95% (does not inactivate some endospores)	
Sterilization	Boiling, steaming or 100% Autoclave, chemical, or dry heat for recommended time	Chemical for 20 minutes

Chapter-6

GENERAL SURGICAL INSTRUMENTATION

Introduction

Surgical instrumentation is critical to the surgical procedure. The performance of the OR team is enhanced when team members **know** each **instrument** by **name**, how each item is **safely handled**, and how each is used. Preparing the instrument for appropriate processing will prolong its use inpatient care and decreases the costs for repair and replacement.

Classifications of Instruments

As an aid in memorizing instrument names, it is helpful to know the basic categories of instruments. They are classified according to their function, and most fall into one of four groups.

A. Cutting and Dissecting

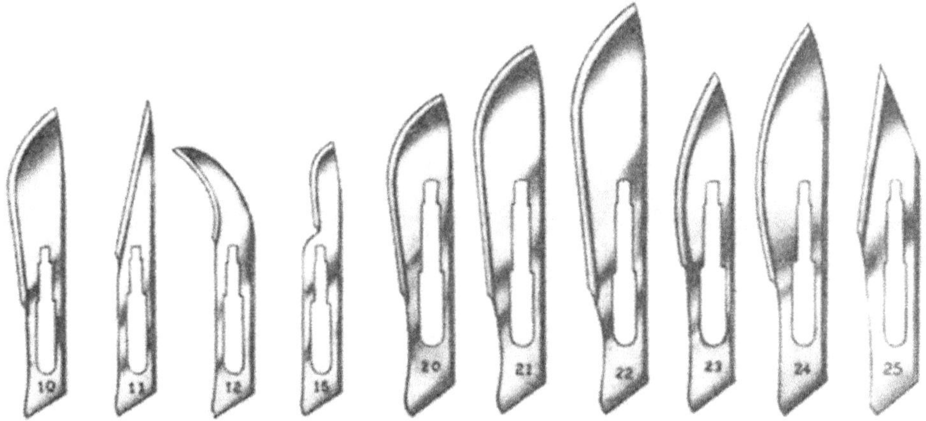

Fig. 1. *Different size surgical blades*

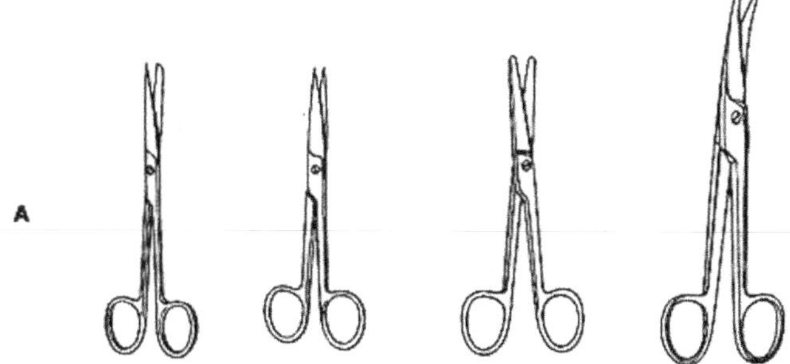

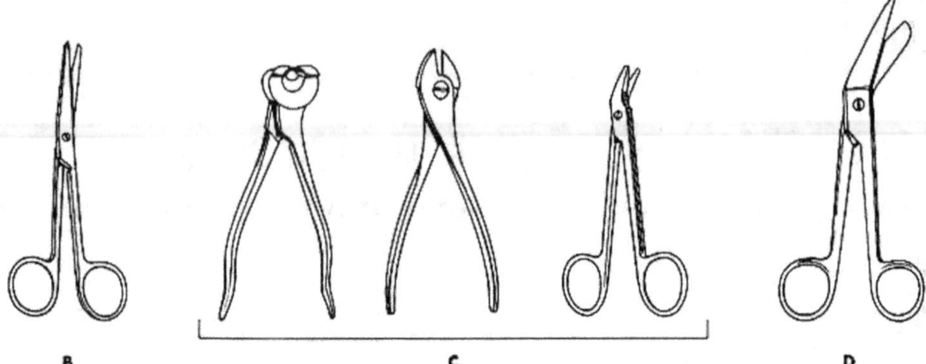

Fig. 2. *Scissors:* *A. Tissue scissors. Blades may be straight or curved and either pointed/blunt, pointed/ pointed, or blunt/blunt. B. Suture scissors. C. Wire cutters and scissors. D. Dressing/bandage scissor*

B. Grasping and Clamping

A clamp is an instrument that clasps tissue between its jaws. Clamps are available for use on nearly every type of body tissue, from delicate eye muscle to heavy bone. The most common clamps are the haemostatic clamps, designed to grasp blood vessels, crushing clamps, non-crushing vascular clamps etc.

Grasping instruments are used to hold and manipulate structures. Needle holder, thumb forceps, tissue forceps, Alli's forceps, bone holders, tenaculi (tenaculm, singular) etc.

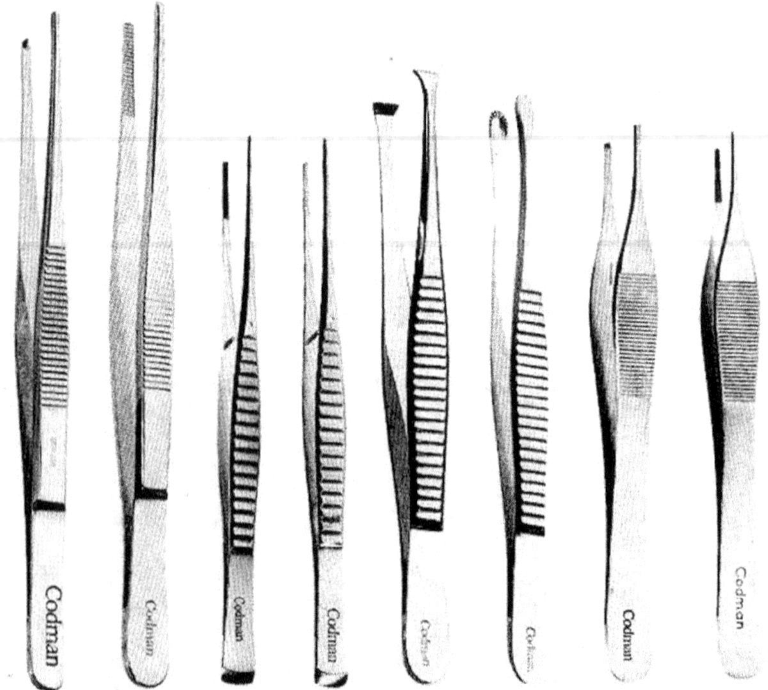

Fig. 3. *Different types of thumb forceps*

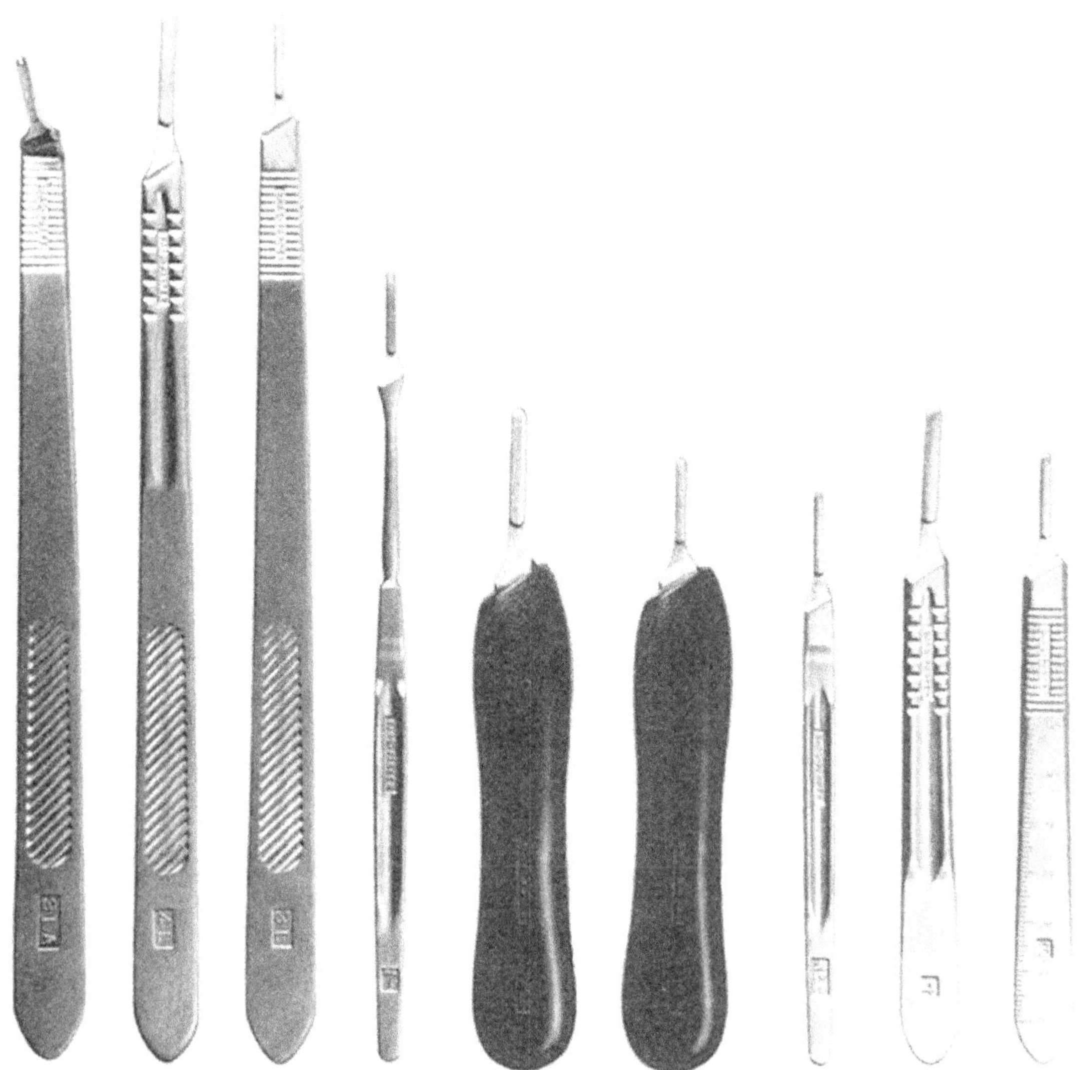

Fig. 4. *Different types of blade holders (scalpel handles*

C. Exposing and Retracting

Soft tissues, muscles, and other structures should be pulled aside for exposure of the surgical site. Exposing and retracting instruments are those that hold tissue or organs away from the area where the surgeon is working. Retractors, like clamps, are available for use in all parts of the body. They may be very shallow, as for skin retraction, or very deep, as for the retraction of abdominal contents. Retractors can be handheld or self-retaining.

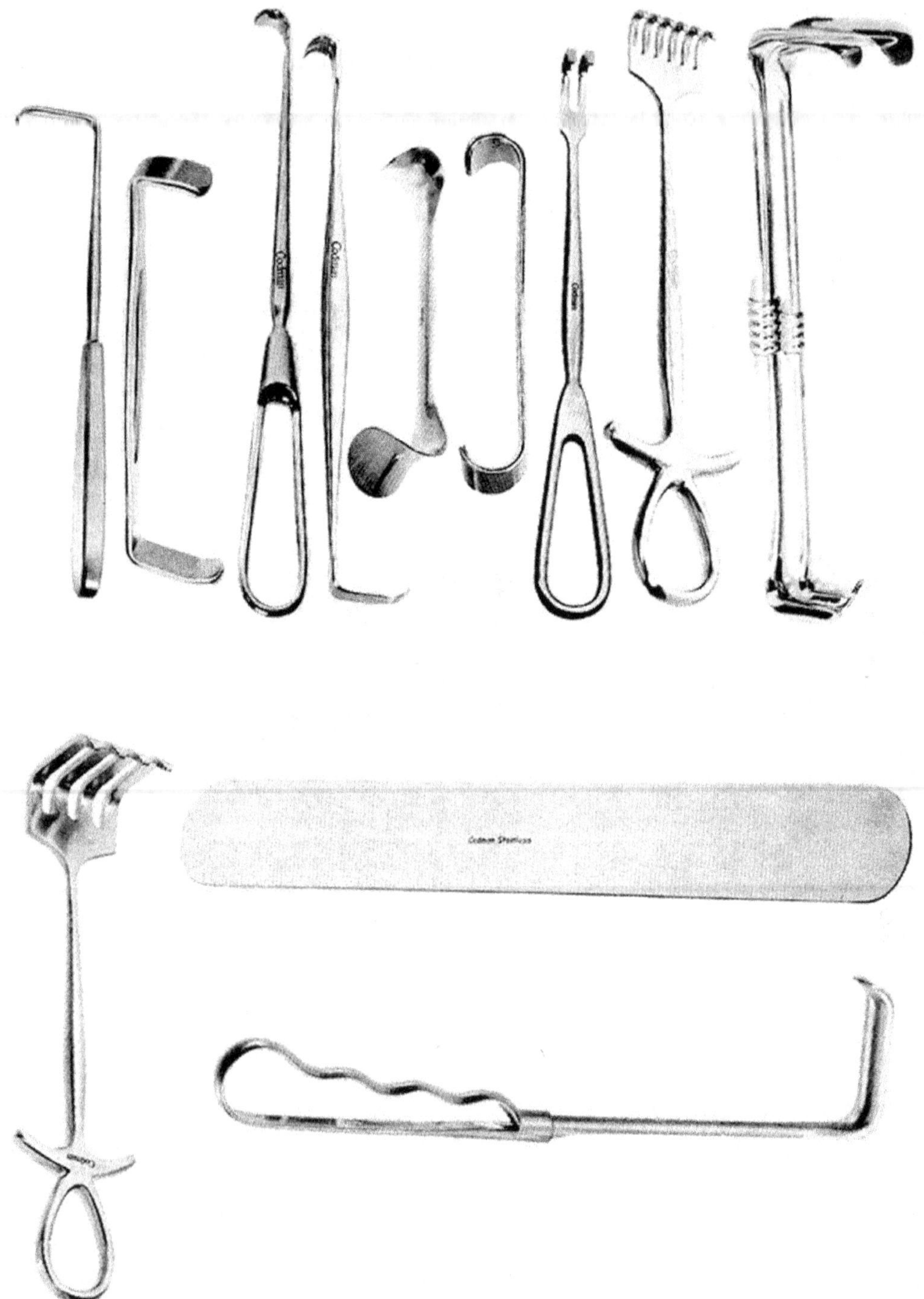

Fig. 5. *Different types of handheld retractors*

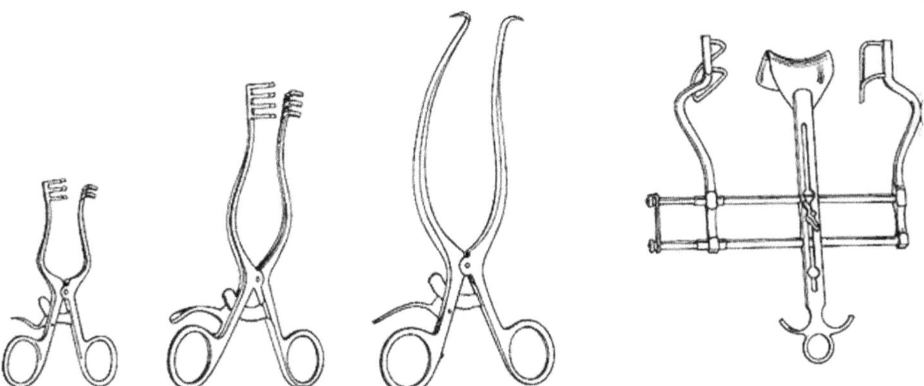

Fig. 6. *Different types of self-retaining retractors*

D. Probing and Dilating

A probe is used to explore a structure or to locate an obstruction. Probes are used to explore the depth of a wound or to trace the path of a fistula. Dilators are used to increase/enlarge the diameter of a lumen, such as the urethra, uterinecervix, or esophagus.

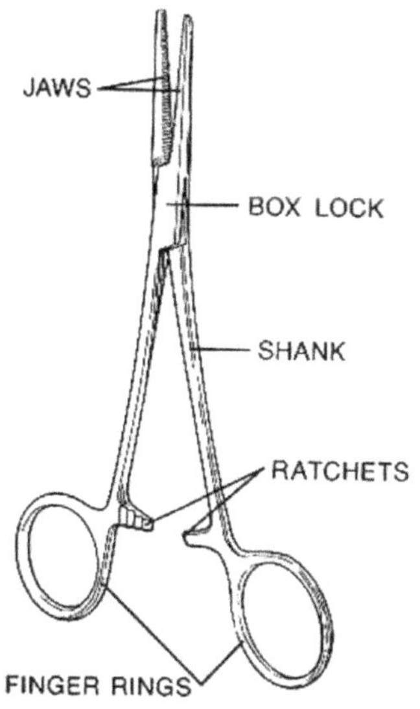

Fig. 7.

Recommendations for Inclusion in Local Policy

The three main areas for consideration are:

- Care of instruments
- General safeguards
- Storage of instruments.

A. Care of Instruments

- Staff involved in the cleaning and packing process of instruments must use standard blood and body substance isolation precautions.
- In order to prevent damage, instruments must only be used for the purpose for which they are designed.
- Proper selection requires a general understanding of surgical procedures and a knowledge of anatomy.
- In order to prevent corrosions or damage, instruments must not be immersed in saline, hypochlorite, and chemical disinfectants.
- To prevent damage, delicate instruments should be handled with care and separated from other instruments.
- Specialized instruments should be regularly checked by an appropriately trained person. Specialist equipment should be made available to check the integrity of diathermy cables and instruments.

B. General Safeguards

- Regular inspection of all instruments should be made by an appropriately qualified person.

- In order to maintain asepsis, instruments found to be contaminated with dried blood or body tissue prior to surgery must be discarded. If found on a tray of instruments, the whole tray must be discarded and the incident reported to the appropriate person.

- If, on opening a tray of instruments, any areas are damp or drops of moisture are observed, the whole tray must be discarded and the incident reported.

- Each tray of instruments should contain an instrument checklist, which incorporates the information necessary for a recorded program of use.

- The scrub person should ensure that instruments are handled in such a manner as to avoid personal injury, injury to the patient or to other members of the surgical team.

- Special care should be taken with sharp instruments (*e.g.*, scalpels and loaded needle holders). It is strongly recommended that all sharp instruments are transferred between staff in a receiver.

- Instruments must not be allowed to rest directly on the patient, which could cause injury to the patient and damages to the drapes.

- Instruments which have been taken directly from an autoclave into the operating room must be allowed to cool naturally before use.

C. *Storage of Instruments*

- The storage area should be clean, dry and free of dust.

- All storage surfaces should be smooth, non-porous and be easily cleanable.

- Sterile items should be protected from direct sunlight.

- The temperature of the storage areas should have a relative humidity of 35% to 68%.

- Perioperative personnel should have the knowledge and skills related to the handling of sterile items.

- Sterile items should be transferred to and from storage areas on clean, specifically designated trolleys.

- All sterile items should have an event related shelf life. The length of time an item can be considered sterile is referred to as the shelf life.

SUTURE USED IN OPEARATION THEARTE

Location/Use	Material	Size
Blood vessels/ Ligation	Chromic gut	3-0 to 0
	Cotton	3-0 to 0
	Silk	3-0 to 1
	Polyester	5-0 to 0
Blood vessels/ Anastomosis	Silk	7-0 to 2-0
	Polyester	6-0 to 2-0
	Polyethylene	6-0 to 4-0
Biliary system	Chromic gut	3-0 to 0
	Cotton	3-0 to 0
	Silk	3-0 to 0
	Polyester	4-0 to 0
Bone/Approximate	Stainless steel	3-0 to 0
	Polyester	3-0 to 0
	Polyethylene	4-0 to 0

Location/Use	Material	Size
Breast	Chromic gut	3-0 to 0
	Silk	3-0 to 0
	Polyester	3-0 to 0
Bronchus/Ligation	Chromic gut	0 to 1
	Silk	3-0 to 0
	Polyester	3-0 to 0
Cleft palate	Nylon	3-0 to 2-0
	Silk	3-0
	Polyester	3-0, 4-0
Dura mater	Silk	6-0 to 4-0
	Polyester	6-0 to 4-0
Eye/Cataract	Chromic gut	7-0, 6-0
	Silk	9-0 to 4-0
	Nylon	10-0 to 9-0

Location/Use	Material	Size	Location/Use	Material	Size
Eye/Muscle repair	Dacron	5-0	Nerve/Repair	Silk	9-0 to 4-0
	Chromic gut	6-0 to 4-0		Nylon	9-0 to 4-0
	Plain gut	6-0 to 4-0		Polyethylene	6-0 to 4-0
	Polyester	5-0		Stainless steel	9-0, 6-0
Eye/Lid	Silk	6-0 to 4-0		Polyester	7-0 to 5-0
	Polyester	6-0, 5-0	Pancreas	Cotton	3-0
Fascia	Chromic gut	2-0 to 1		Silk	3-0
	Silk	2-0 to 0	Perineum	Chromic gut	4-0 to 3-0
	Stainless steel	4-0 to 3-0	Peritoneum	Chromic gut	3-0 to 0
	Polyester	2-0 to 0		Silk	4-0 to 1
	Cotton	2-0, 0		Cotton	3-0 to 0
Heart	Silk	6-0 to 2		Plain gut	0
	Polyester	5-0 to 0		Polyester	3-0 to 2-0
Hernia/Repair	Chromic gut	3-0 to 1	Rectum	Chromic gut	4-0 to 0
	Cotton	2-0 to 1	Skin	Nylon	6-0 to 2-0
	Silk	3-0 to 0		Polyethylene	5-0 to 3-0
	Polyester	3-0 to 0		Silk	6-0 to 2-0
	Stainless steel	5-0 to 3-0		Polyester	6-0 to 3-0
Intestine	Chromic gut	5-0 to 2-0		Stainless steel	5-0 to 2-0
	Silk	5-0 to 2-0	Skull	Stainless steel	5-0 to 4-0
	Cotton	2-0	Stomach/ Anastomosis	Chromic gut	5-0 to 2-0
Joint capsule	Chromic gut	4-0 to 0		Cotton	3-0 to 0
	Cotton	2-0		Silk	3-0 to 0
	Silk	3-0		Polyester	4-0 to 2-0
	Stainless steel	5-0	Tendon	Stainless steel	5-0 to 3-0
	Polyester	4-0 to 1		Polyester	5-0 to 3-0
Kidney	Chromic gut	4-0		Polyethylene	5-0 to 3-0
	Plain gut	4-0		Nylon	5-0 to 3-0
Lip	Chromic gut	5-0	Thyroid	Chromic gut	3-0 to 0
	Plain gut	5-0		Cotton	3-0 to 0
Liver	Silk	2-0, 0		Silk	3-0 to 0
	Chromic gut	2-0, 0		Polyester	3-0 to 0
Muscle	Plain gut	3-0 to 0	Tonsil	Plain gut	3-0 to 0
	Chromic gut	3-0 to 0	Ureter	Chromic gut	4-0
	Cotton	3-0 to 0	Urethra	Chromic gut	4-0
	Silk	3-0 to 0	Uterus	Chromic gut	2-0 to 0
	Polyester	3-0 to 0			

Chapter-7

RECEIVING AND POSITIONING THE PATIENT

Introduction

The patient is the reason for the existence of the healthcare team. She or he looks to the operating room team to fulfill her or his diverse needs during the pre-, intra-, and postoperative phases of care. The patient is always the focus of attention, not just when she or he is under the operating room (OR) spotlight. The operating room team, therefore, is expected to practice the details mentioned below:

When we receive the patient:

- Greet the patient by name and introduce yourself and explain the purpose of coming to the OR.

- Review the patient's chart for completeness.

- Obtain information by asking about the patient's understanding of the surgical procedure.

- Check whether all preoperative preparations havebeen done.

- Answer the patient's questions about the surgical procedure.

- Encourage the patient and his/her family to discuss their feelings or anxieties regarding the surgical procedure and anticipated results.

- Identify any special needs of the patient that will alter the plan for intraoperative care.

- Offer the patient psychological reassurance and maintain an attitude of hope. Avoid using phrases such as, "Everything will be all right" or "You are okay." Reinforce the concept that the team will provide good care.

- By fulfilling spiritual and psychosocial needs, the caregiver helps to provide the preoperative patient with as much peace of mind as possible. Understandably, the patient's tension level rises as the time for the surgical procedure approaches.

- The better prepared the patient is emotionally, the smoother his/her postoperative course will be.

- Generally, the impact inherent in any type of surgical intervention can be reconciled when the patient has hope and confidence in the caregivers to relieve fear and provide security.

- Preoperative preparations can influence the outcome of the surgical procedure.

Positioning the Patient

Each operative position represents an agreement between the surgeon and the anaesthesia provider to the patient. The surgeon requires an accessible, stable operative area. The anaesthesia provider must have space in which to administer the anaesthetic and free flowing intravenous. The result must come well within the rules for maximum safety and comfort to the patient.

Preliminary Considerations

Proper positioning for a surgical procedure is a facet of patient care. This is as important to patient outcome as adequate preoperative preparation and safe anaesthesia.

Proper positioning requires a knowledge of anatomy and the application of physiologic principles, as well as familiarity with the necessary equipment. Safety is a primary consideration.

Patient positioning is determined by the procedure to be performed, with consideration given to the surgeon's choice of surgical approach and the technique of anaesthetic administration. Factors such as age, height, weight, cardiopulmonary status, and preexisting disease (*e.g.*, arthritis) also influence positioning and should be incorporated into the plan of care. Preoperatively, the patient should be assessed for:

- Alterations in skin integrity
- Joint mobility
- The presence of joint or vascular prostheses.

The expected outcome is that the patient will not be harmed by positioning for surgical procedure.

Responsibility for Patient Positioning

The choice of position for a surgical procedure is made by the surgeon in consultation with the anaesthesia provider. Adjustments are made as necessary for the administration of anaesthetic and for maintenance of the patient's physiology. In essence, patient positioning is a shared responsibility among all team members. The anaesthesia provider has the final wordon positioning when the patient's physiologic status and monitoring is in question.

Timing of Patient Positioning and Anaesthetic Administration

The following states the time at which the patient is positioned and/or anaesthetized.

- After transfer from the stretcher to the operating bed, the patient is usually placed face up on his/her back (supine).

- The patient may either be anaesthetized in this position and then positioned for the surgical procedure or first positioned and then anaesthetized.
- If the patient is aving a procedure performed while in a face down (prone) position and under general anaesthesia, he/she is anaesthetized and intubated on the transport stretcher.
- A minimum of four people are required to place the patient safely in the prone position on the operating bed.

Several factors influence the time at which the patient is positioned. Some of these include:

- The site of the surgical procedure
- The age and size of the patient
- The technique of anaesthetic administration and
- If the patient is conscious, has pain on moving.

Remember that the patient is not positioned or moved until the anaesthesia provider indicates it is safe to do so.

Preparation for Positioning

Before the patient is brought to the operating room (OR), the circulating nurse should do the following:

- Review the proposed position by referring to the surgeon's preference in the patient's chart.
- Ask for assistance if unsure how to position the patient.
- Consult the surgeon as soon as she/he arrives if not sure which position is to be used.
- Check the working part of the operating bed before bringing the patient into the room.
- Assemble all attachments and protective pads anticipated for the surgical procedure.

- Test positioning devices for patient safety. Check for cleanliness.
- Review the plan of care for unique needs of the patient.

Safety Measures

Injuries to the back, arms, or shoulders as a result of lifting patients or moving equipment are common to the staff working in the OR. Several principles of body mechanics (using the body as a machine) should be observed to minimize physical injury.

Some of these principles include, but are not limited to the following:

- Keep the body as close as possible to the person or equipment to be lifted or moved while maintaining a straight back.
- Lift with the large muscle groups of the legs and abdominal muscles, not the back.
- Lift with a slow, even motion, keeping pressure off the lumbar (lower back) area.
- Bend forward with hip flexion and hand support.

Safety measures, including the following, are observed while transferring, moving, and positioning patients:

- The patient is properly identified before being transferred to the operating bed and the surgical site is affirmed.
- The patient is assessed for mobility status.
- The operating bed and transport vehicle are securely locked in position, with the mattress stabilized during transfer to and from the operating bed.
- Two persons should assist an awake patient with the transfer by positioning themselves on each side of the patient.
- Adequate assistance in lifting unconscious, obese, or weak patients is necessary to prevent injury.
- The anaesthesia provider guards the head of the anaesthetized patient at all times and support it during movement.
- The anaesthetized patient is not moved without permission of the anaesthesia provider. He/she is moved slowly and gently to allow the control of airway and circulatory system during movement.
- No body part should extend beyond the edges of the operating bed or contact metal parts or unpadded surfaces.
- Body exposure should be minimal to prevent hypothermia and to preserve dignity.
- Movement and positioning.

Anatomic and physiologic considerations

A patient's tolerance of the stresses of the surgical procedure depends greatly on normal functioning of the vital systems of the body. The patient's physical condition is considered, and proper body alignment is important. Criteria are met for physiologic positioning to prevent injury from pressure, obstruction, or stretching.

Accessibility of the Surgical Site

The surgical procedure and patient condition determine the position in which the patient is placed. To minimize trauma and operating time, the surgeon must have adequate exposure of the surgical site.

Accessibility for Anaesthetic Administration

The anaesthesia provider should be able to attach monitoring electrodes, administer the anesthetic process and observe its effects, and maintain IV access. The patient's airway is of prime concern and must be patent and accessible at all times.

Individual Positioning Considerations

- If a patient is extremely obese, his/her arms may be placed on armboards.

- Patients with joint problems may need special individualized care because of limited range of motion in their joints.
- A patient who has cardiac problems or is obese may experience orthopnea or dyspnea when lying flat.

Equipment for Positioning

The following are list of special equipment for positioning a surgical patient:

- Shoulder Bridge (Thyroid Elevator)
- Safety Belt (Thigh Strap)
- Anaesthesia Screen
- Lift Sheet (Draw Sheet)
- Armboard, double Armboard
- Wrist or Arm Strap
- Shoulder Braces or Supports
- Body Rests and Braces
- Kidney Rests
- Body (Hip) Restraint Strap
- Metal Footboard
- Headrests
- Pressure-minimizing Mattress
- Operating Bed.

Surgical Positioning

The position in which the patient is placed on the operating bed/table depends on the surgical procedure to be performed as well as on the physical condition of the patient.

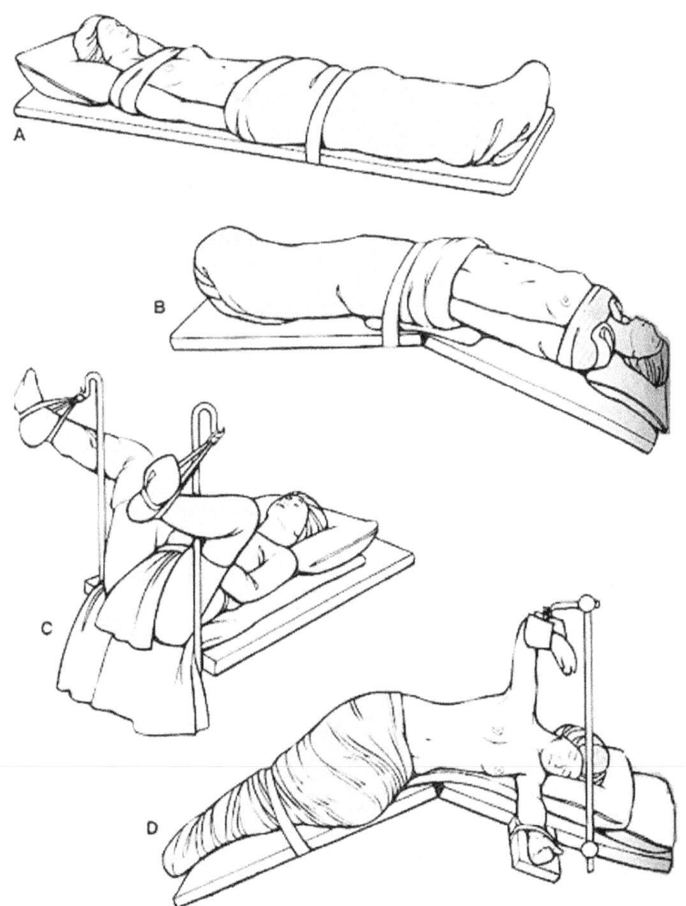

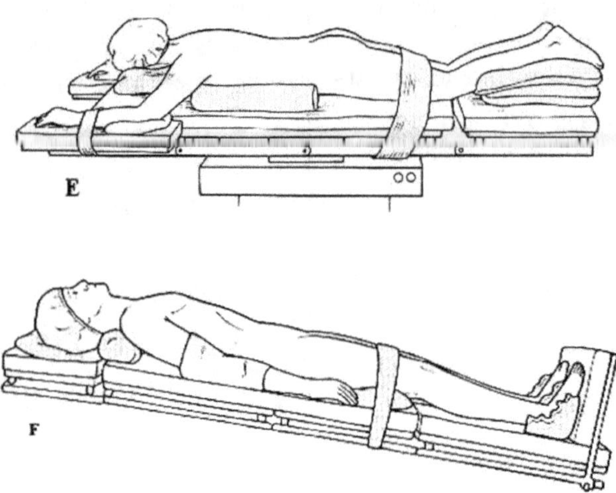

Fig. 1. *Positioning on the operating table; (A) Supine, (B) Trendelenburg, (C) Lithotomy, (D) modified Sim's/ Kidney position. (E) Prone position (F) Reverse Trendelenburg position*

The patient should be in a comfortable position whether asleep or awake.

- The operative area must be adequately exposed.

- The vascular supply should not be obstructed by awkward position or undue pressure on a part.

- There should be no interference with the patient's respiration as a result of pressure of the arms on the chest or constriction of the neck or chest caused by a gown.

- Nerves must be protected from undue pressure. Improper positioning of the arms, hands, legs, or feet may cause serious injury or paralysis.

- Precautions for patient safety must be observed, particularly with thin, elderly, or obese patients.

- The patient needs gentle restraint before induction, incase of excitement.

Many positions are used for surgical procedures; the most commonly used positions are listed below.

A. Dorsal recumbent (supine) position

- The usual position for surgery is flat on the back.

- One arm is at the side of the bed/table, with the hand placed palm down.

- The other is carefully positioned on an armboard for intravenous infusion.

B. Trendelenburg Position

- Usually used for surgery on the lower abdomen and the pelvis to obtain good exposure by displacing the intestines into the upper abdomen.

- In this position, the head and body are lowered and the knees are flexed.

- The patient is held in position by padded shoulder braces.

C. Lithotomy Position

- In this position, the patient is lying on the back with the legs and thighs flexed at right angles.

- The position is maintained by placing the feet in stirrups.

- Nearly all perineal, rectal, and vaginal surgical procedures require this position.

D. For Kidney Surgery

The patient is placed on the non-operative side in Sim's position with an air pillow 12.5 to 15 cm thick under the loin, or on a table with a kidney or back lift.

E. Prone position

Patient lies on abdomen. Chest rolls under axillae and sides of chest to iliac crests raise body weight from chest to facilitate respiration; pillow under feet protects toes.

F. Reverse Trendelenburg

Reverse Trendelenburg position, with soft roll under shoulders for thyroid, neck, or shoulder procedures.

G. For Chest and Abdominothoracic Surgery

The position varies with the surgery to be performed. The surgeon and the anaesthesia provider place the patient on the operating table/bed in the desired position.

H. Surgery on the Neck

Neck surgery, for example, surgery involving the thyroid, is performed with the patient on the back, the neck extended somewhat by a pillow beneath the shoulders, and the head and chest elevated to reduce venous pressure.

I. Surgery on the Skull and the Brain

Such procedures demand special positions and apparatus, usually adjusted by the surgeon.

Modifications for Individual Patient Needs

As with everything else, the patient's individual needs are met during positioning. Anomalies and physical defects are considered. Whether the patient is unconscious or conscious, the avoidance of unnecessary exposure is an essential consideration for all patients. The patient's position should be observed objectively before skin preparation and draping to see that it adheres to physiologic principles. Protective devices, positioning aids, and padded areas should be reassessed before draping, because they could have shifted during the skin preparation procedure or during insertion of an indwelling urinary catheter.

Chapter-8

PREPARATION AND DRAPING OF THE SURGICAL SITE

Introduction

The surgeon, assistants for the surgeon, the scrub nurse, as well as the patient, must have a preoperative surgical scrub. The patient must also be covered with sterile linen leaving the incision site open. While the solutions used for the patient's skin preparation may vary in different hospitals, basic principles remain the same. Likewise, draping materials vary somewhat, but draping principles are universal.

Purpose

The purpose of skin preparation is to render the surgical site as free as possible from transient and resident microorganisms, dirt, and skin oil so that the incision can be made through the skin with minimal danger of infection from this source.

The Trim Preparation

Hair readily supports the growth of microorganisms and therefore, the skin at and around the incision site is trimmed immediately prior to surgery.

Procedure for Trimming

1. Explain the procedure to the patient.
2. Assemble needed supplies before beginning.
3. Be sure to have good lighting.
4. Trim the hair to its minimum size.
5. Talk with the patient as you work as this helps to reduce anxiety or embarrassment.
6. Wash the trimmed area thoroughly.

The Scrub Preparation

After the patient is anaesthetized and/or positioned on the operating bed, the skin at the surgical site and an extensive area surrounding it is mechanically cleansed again with an antiseptic agent immediately before draping. Agents such as iodine, iodophore, alcohol can be used.

Procedure

1. Expose the site and adjust light. Check the trim prep.
2. Don (wear) sterile gloves.
3. Place sterile towels at the periphery of the scrub area.
4. Starting at the incision site, begin washing in a circular motion.
5. Repeat the process.
6. Dry the prep area using the same technique with dry sponges.
7. Antiseptic paint is usually applied immediately after the scrub.
8. Scrub and paint solutions should be chemically similar.

Skin Preparation for Specific Anatomic Areas

Eye

- Never shave/trim the eyebrows; the eyelashes may be trimmed.
- Use soft cotton balls.
- Irrigate from the inner to the outer canthus.

- Use nonirritating antiseptic agents.
- The conjunctival sac is flushed with nontoxic agent (normal saline).
- The ear on the affected side should be plugged with cotton.

Ear

- Clean folds with cotton tipped applicators.
- Prevent pooling of solution in the ear canal.

Face

- Has several unclean areas (the mouth, nose, and hairline).
- Difficult to avoid contaminating the prep when the usual technique is employed.
- Prep from the center outwards (from hairline).
- Return to the incision site using clean sponges and prep that area last.
- Braid, cap or held back the hair with clips prior to the prep.

Flat surfaces—abdomen

- Follow the prep guidelines.
- Use cotton tip applicators to remove dead skin from the umbilicus.
- If colostomy is present place a soapy sponge over it.
- Prep the colostomy last.

Elevated limb

- Place a moisture-proof pad on the operating bed under the elevated extremity to protect the operating bed.
- Elevate and support the extremity until sterile drapes are applied.
- Begin the prep at the most elevated point, rather than at the incision site.

Breast for biopsy

- Do it very gently.
- Prevent spreading of cancer cells.

Vagina

- Begin a few centimeters from the vulva.
- Extend the prep outwards to include the thighs and lower abdomen.
- Sponge sticks are used to prep the vagina itself. To complete the prep wash the vulva and anus and passing the soapy sponge downward.
- Discard the sponge after it passes the anus.
- Repeat several times, always starting with a new sponge.

Anus

- Is considered as a contaminated area.
- Prep the surrounding area first and the anus itself last.

Documentation

Details of the preoperative skin condition and preparation should be documented in the patient's intra-operative record.

Drapes and Draping

Drapes are pieces of cloth used to cover areas in order to provide sterile field, protective barrier against contamination and moisture.

Draping, on the other hand, is the process of covering the patient and surrounding areas with sterile linen, leaving only a minimum area of skin exposed at the site of surgical site.

Purpose of Draping

The purpose of draping is to create and maintain an adequate sterile field during the operative procedure. However, drapes should not be larger than necessary, as they cause the patient to perspire excessively.

Responsibility

- While the surgeon is putting on gown and gloves, the assistant is scrubbing the patient.
- The surgeon and his/her assistant(s) usually place the towels and towel clips to outline the site of incision.

Points Concerning Drapes

- When packaged for sterilization, drapes must be properly folded and arranged.
- They must be free from holes. If a hole is found in a drape, after it is laid down, the hole must be covered with another piece of linen, or the entire drape should be discarded.
- While it is the responsibility of the person who folds the linen to see it is free from holes, occasionally all the holes may not be detected.

Basic Principles of Draping

- Provide a wide cuff for the hand. This prevents contamination of the hand by the non-sterile surface being draped.
- Drapes are nearly always unfolded at the field to avoid moving them around.
- Once laced, drapes should not be moved. Moving a drape after it is placed causes bacteria from unprepared surface to contaminate the draped incisional site illustrates the placement of drapes over the incisional area and shows the cuff that protects the hand.
- When linen drapes are used, provide adequate barriers against moisture and contamination.

Draping Materials and their Application

Towels

These are usually the basic items in every draping routine. Four towels are placed around the immediate surgical site; this is called "squaring off" the site. Four towel clips secure the towels. These clips may penetrate the skin and towels together or simply join the towels. Some surgeons prefer to sew the drapes to the skin.

Draped Patient

Four towels secured with towel clips mark the boundary of the incision site. This is also called a minor sheet, top sheet, or bottom sheet.

It is a large rectangular sheet that may be placed directly above or below the incisional area. It is used in various ways in the draping routine, according to its size.

Plastic Drape

- This is a commercially prepared item.
- Its function is to provide a sterile barrier over the skin at the incisional site.
- Two or three people are needed to place the drape.
- The sheet is made of thin plastic that is adherent on one side.
- Some surgeons feel that this type of barrier causes a greater proliferation of bacteria since it increases the perspiration and warmth of the skin it covers.
- The surgeon and his/her first assistant hold the drape taut, while the second assistant pulls the paper from the adhesive side.
- The sheet is then lowered onto the patient and smoothed down.

In addition to the above mentioned materials, there are different kinds of procedure sheets designed to fit the needs of a particular surgical position or type of surgery. The sheet may have fenestration (hole) or other access to the incisional site. The fenestration must usually be larger than the incisional site.

Draping Rules

- Handle drapes as little as possible.
- Never flourish drapes. Dust and lint are then released into the air, creating a vehicle for airborne bacteria.
- If a drape becomes contaminated or has a hole in it, discard it.
- Never allow gloved hands to come into contact with the patient's prepared skin during the draping process. The gloved hands are sterile, but the skin is not.
- Whenever draping, always provide a cuff for the gloved hand.
- Never allow a drape to extend outside the sterile area, unless it is to remain there. The drape must not be adjusted once it is placed. If it is placed incorrectly, it must be discarded and another drape must be used.
- Do not allow the drapes to touch the floor or become tangled in floor equipment.
- If the drape is so large that it touches the floor, the bottom may be taped to form a make shift item.
- Plan ahead. Have the drapes ready before the procedure begins.

Areas Affected by Surgical Conscience

Protection of the patient

Patient protection is an area of surgery that is strongly affected by surgical conscience. The operating room team must be aware of the dangers that exist for the patient. Like a defensive driver, the team must be constantly on the lookout for situations that might be harmful to the patient.

A. Electrical hazards are a major risk in the operating room. Hence,

- Cords that are frayed or plugs that appear defective must not be used.

- Whenever the electrocautery is used, the patient must be grounded in order to prevent shock or burns.
- Equipment that malfunctions must be taken out of service as soon as the defect is discovered.

B. Moving and positioning the patient must be carried out with constant attention to:

- Proper padding and protection of bony surfaces
- Prominent nerves
- Blood vessels.

The unconscious patient cannot safeguard him/herself and is therefore, in greater need of vigilance on the part of others. Operating team members must see and feel for the patient by being alert at all times. Side rails must be raised as soon as the patient is moved to the stretcher or bed, and restraint or safety straps must be applied on the operating bed.

C. Environmental protection, in the form of warmth and comfort.

- Is essential in patient care.
- Unnecessary exposure of the patient's body should not be allowed.
- Care for the dignity of the patient, regardless of age or condition, should be observed at all times.

D. Protection from psychological insult is the responsibility of everyone in the operating room. The patient must not be allowed to overhear or misinterpret matters discussed that are intended to be confidential or are offensive. The patient must be made to feel that his/her well-being is the primary concern of all those around him/her.

E. Anxiety and **fear** accompany nearly every patient in the operating room. Even though preoperative medications are effective in controlling anxiety, they cannot replace the warm touch or understanding voice of a staff member.

F. Unnecessary time spent under anaesthesia because of poor planning show poor surgical conscience. Attention to detail before the case begins will prevent loss of time during the case. The operating room team members should anticipate as much as possible the instruments or special equipment that will be needed for the case.

- Fears and pain are very real and should be treated strongly.
- Respect for the patient's right to privacy is absolutely mandatory.
- The patient must not be discussed outside the operating room where friends and relatives might overhear and misinterpret information.
- The patient's condition is a private matter between him/herself and the healthcare providers. It is not the topic for public discussion.

Reporting of an incident, in the operating room, is a major ethical responsibility. An occurrence such as a major break in technique, medication error, or any event that violates operating room policy is considered an incident.

Honesty, of course, is a major ethical standard. It is more important to admit that a procedure or activity is unfamiliar than to proceed blindly in order to save face. It follows that the operating room nurse or any staff member must be honest about his/her own capabilities so that error can be reduced.

Situations that Undermine Surgical Conscience

While most graduates of surgery programs and experienced personnel are anxious to provide the best patient care possible and to possess a firm surgical conscience, there are factors that can cause one with a good attitude to become apathy. Every professional in the medical field should be on the lookout for apathtic and its causes since it greatly reduces the quality of patient care and safety.

Peer Apathy

When many of those of the operating staff become less attentive to the detail, other staff members may feel, "No one else cares, so why should I? This devastating situation can cause the whole department to lose sight of its primary goal (the patient's safety and protection).

Stress, fatigue, poor health

These factors can certainly affect a person's awareness of his/her responsibilities to the patient. The cause of the situation should be investigated by the staff members concerned, and a solution should be sought.

Personal problems

Any team member who has personal problems is to be preoccupied with it and consequently neglect the patient's safety to some degree. If practical, a short leave of absence or counselling may be necessary.

Staff relations

It is common for surgery personnel to work better with some surgeons than with others. There are, of course, some surgeons with whom all nursing and other team members are pleased to work with. Regardless of the surgeon, however, attention to patient safety and ethical responsibilities should not change. It must not be the personality of the surgeon that dictates the quality of care given to the patient.

Chapter-9

PRINCIPLES OF ANAESTHESIA

Introduction

Anaesthesiology is the branch of medicine that is concerned with the administration of medication or anaesthetic agent to relieve pain and support physiologic function during a surgical procedure. The American Board of Anaesthesiology has defined anaesthesiology as the practice of medicine dealing with the management of procedures for rendering a patient insensible to pain during surgical procedures, and with the support of life functions under the stress of anaesthetic and surgical manipulations.

Anaesthesia, the absence of sensation, may be produced in a specific body area or systemically. When the agent given causes unconsciousness, the anaesthetic is termed general (general anaesthesia) when an agent is directed into a specific area to cause analgesia, the absence of pain, it is called conductive or local or regional Anaesthesia.

Types of Anaesthesia

Local anaesthesia

The agent used during local anaesthesia acts on a single nerve, a group of nerves or on superficial nerve endings. During all types of local/regional anaesthesia including local infiltration, nerve block, topical, epidural and spinal, the patient remains conscious.

Local infiltration

- The agent is injected intracutaneously and subcutaneously into tissues at and around the incisional site to block peripheral sensory nerve stimuli at their origin. The surgery should not be extensive.

- It is used to suture superficial lacerations or for excision of minor lesions.

- Addition of Adrenaline (Epinephrine) to the anaesthetic agent causes vasoconstriction to slow circulatory uptake and absorption, thus prolonging anaesthesia.

- Use a calibrated syringe to avoid over dosage.

- The patient receiving Adrenaline should be well oxygenated.

- Agents with Adrenaline are contraindicated for operative procedures involving fingers and penis.

- High levels of local anaesthetic are toxic.

- Administration of it takes place as part of the sterile procedure - use sterile needle and syringe.

- When highly vascularized areas are to be injected, epinephrine is sometimes added to the anaesthetic (to minimize local bleeding, prolong the effect of the agent).

Nerve block

- Anaesthesia of a large single nerve or nerves.

- Injection is done not necessarily at the immediate surgical site.
- Commonly used in surgery that is performed on fingers and toes.
- The supplying nerve is anaesthetized.

Topical

- Used to numb superficial nerve endings particularly those of the mucous membranes.
- The agent may be—swabbed, sprayed or applied in drops as for eye surgery.
- Useful in preparing the patient for endoscopic procedures, such as bronchoscopy and esophagoscopy.

Regional Anaesthesia

Epidural

- Introduced into the epidural space of the spine.
- The agent baths the nerve roots of the spinal cord and the area supplied by these nerves is anaesthetized.
- The anaesthetic is injected outside the spinal canal (no direct contact between spinal fluid and anaesthetic).

Caudal

- Type of epidural anaesthesia.
- Directed into the caudal canal at the sacrum.
- Ideal for obstetrics and procedures on the perineum.

Spinal

- Introduction of the anaesthetic into the subarachnoid space at the fourth or fifth lumbar inter space.
- Here the agent does come into contact with the spinal fluid Ideal for surgery of the lower pelvis, such as cesarean section or hernia repair; lower extremities.

Risk of infection in the spinal canal if the puncture site and/or the plastic tube, etc. is contaminated.

Adverse reactions to local anaesthesia

Proper monitoring of blood pressure, pulse rate, and heart rhythm is essential. Monitor the patient every 15 minutes during the procedure. All team members should be aware of the danger signals that accompany an adverse reaction. Adverse reaction occurs when the patient receives overdose, which is by far the most common complication. Relative overdose occurs when the patient receives too much anaesthetic too quickly, as when a vein or artery is punctured during the administration of the anaesthetic. The anaesthetic travels quickly to the brain and the following symptoms may be observed:

- **Stimulation:** Patient may become very talkative or anxious, signs of tachycardia thready pulse, convulsion.
- **Depression:** Patient may appear sleepy and unresponsive, bradycardia, hypo tension.
- **Other signs:** Patient may develop cyanosis, sweating feel cold, act restless (signs of shock). Fainting, itching, nausea or sudden headache may also occur.

Treatment of the Reaction

- Discontinue the anaesthetic immediately.
- Oxygen administration may be needed.
- Cardiopulmonary resuscitation is initiated, if necessary.

Generic Name	Trade Name(s)	Uses	Concentration	Duration of Effect (Hours)	Maximum Dosage
Amino Amides					
Bupivacaine hydrochloride	Marcaine Sensorcaine	Local infiltration Regional block Surgical epidural	0.25% to 0.50%	2 to 3	400 mg
Dibucaine hydrochloride	Nupercaine Percaine Cinchocaine	Local infiltration Peripheral nerves	0.05% to 0.1%	3 to 3½	30 mg
Etidocaine hydrochloride	Duranest	Peripheral nerves Epidural	0.5% to 1%	2 to 3	500 mg
Lidocaine hydrochloride	Xylocaine Lignocaine	Topical Infitration Peripheral nerves Nerve block Spinal Epidural	2% to 4% 0.5% 1% to 2%	½ to 2	200 mg 500 mg or 7 mg/kg body weight
Mepivacaine hydrochloride	Carbocaine	Infiltration Peripheral nerves Epidural	0.5% to 1% 1% to 2%	½ to 2	500 mg
Prilocaine hydrochloride	Citanest	Infiltration Peripheral nerves Regional block Epidural	1% to 2% 2% to 3%	½ to 2½	600 mg
Amino Esters					
Chloroprocaine hydrochloride	Nesacaine	Infiltration Peripheral nerves Nerve block Epidural	0.5% 2% 2% 2% to 3%	¼ to ½	1000 mg
Cocaine hydrochloride		Topical	4% or 10%	½	200 mg or 4 mg/kg body weight
Procaine hydrochloride	Novocaine	Infiltration Peripheral nerves Spinal	0.5% 1% to 2%	¼ to ½	1000 mg or 14 mg/kg body weight
Tetracaine hydrochloride	Cetacaine Pontocaine	Topical Spinal	2% 1%	2 to 4	20 mg

General Anaesthesia

- Causes unconsciousness, provides analgesia and muscle relaxation.
- Depending upon the type and amount of agent used, he patient may be slightly or not at all responsive to stimuli.
- A combination of agents is frequently used to achieve the desired level of muscle relaxation and analgesia. There are four stages of general anaesthesia. These are induction, excitement, relaxation and danger.

Induction

- The beginning of administration of the initial agent.
- Lasts until the patient is unconscious.
- During this phase, the patient retains an exaggerated sense of hearing until the last moment.
- For this reason it is mandatory that all personnel in the room remain as quiet as possible during induction.

Excitement

- During this phase, the patient is delirious and sensitive to external stimuli.
- Involuntary muscle activity and struggle may be seen.
- Patient is physiologically unstable.

Relaxation

This phase is the level at which surgery may be performed safely.

- The patient is relaxed, unconscious of pain and is physiologically stable.
- Breathing is steady and automatic.
- This phase ends at its deepest level with respiratory paralysis.

Danger

This stage begins when the amount of agent causes such severe depression of the central nervous system that the patient is in immediate danger of cardiopulmonary arrest. Some common general anaesthetic agents are described in table.

Methods of Administering General Anaesthesia Inhalation

The anaesthesia machine (gas machine annex 4) is used to administer both compressed gas anaesthetics (available in tanks) and volatile liquids that are vapourized within the machine before administration. Since the anaesthesia provider controls all gases that enter the patient's lungs, the machine also conveys oxygen in the proper proportion. The patient receives the anaesthetic-oxygen mixture via:

- The endotrecheal tube that is inserted into the trachea or
- From a mask that fits snugly around the nose and mouth.
- In either case, the tube or mask is connected to the machine by a set of hoses through which the gases flow.

Intravenous (IV) and intramuscular (IM) administrations

Injections are also used in general anaesthesia. Liquid agents may be administered directly into the blood stream. A cannula is inserted into the vein and a continuous intravenous drip is maintained throughout surgery. The cannula/catheter is attached to flexible IV tubing. Solutions such as saline or dextrose in saline are attached to the tubing to keep access to the vein open at all times. Other agents such antibiotics or muscle relaxants may also be given through the IV cannula. Some anaesthetic agents, such as Ketamine, may bead ministered intramuscularly. These agents are usually injected by the anaesthesia provider about 15 minutes prior to surgery.

Generic Name	Trade Name	Administration	Characteristics	Uses
Inhalation Agents Nitrous oxide	—	Inhalation	Inorganic gas; slight potency; pleasant fruitlike odor; nonirritating; non-flammable but supports combustion; poor muscle relaxation	Rapid induction and recovery; short procedures when muscle relaxation unimportant; adjunct to potent agents
Halothane	Fluothane	Inhalation	Halogenated volatile liquid; potent; pleasant odour; non-irritaing; cardio-vascular and respiratory depressant; incomplete muscle relaxation; potentially toxic to liver	Rapid induction; wide spectrum for maintenance; depth of anaesthesia easily altered; rapid reversal
Enflurane	Ethrane	Inhalation	Halogenated ether; potent; some muscle relaxation; respiratory depressant	Rapid induction and recovery; wide spectrum for maintenance
Isoflurane	Forane	Inhalation	Halogenated methyl ether; potent; muscle relaxant; profound respiratory depressant; metabolized in liver	Rapid induction and recovery with minimal after effects; wide spectrum for maintenance

Intravenous Agents				
Thiopental sodium	Pentothal sodium	Intravenous	Barbiturate; potent; short acting with cumulative effect; rapid uptake by circulatory system; no muscle relaxation; respiratory depressant	Rapid induction and recovery; short procedures when muscle relaxation not needed; basal anaesthetic
Methohexital sodium	Brevital	Intravenous	Barbiturate; potent; circulatory and respiratory depressant	Rapid induction; brief anaesthesia
Propofol	Diprivan	Intravenous	Alkylphenol; potent short-acting sedative-hypnotic; cardiovascular depressant	Rapid induction and recovery; short procedure alone; prolonged anaesthesia in combination with inhalation agents or opioids
Ketamine hydrochloride	Ketaject, Ketalar	Intravenous, intramuscular	Dissociative drug; profound amnesia and analgesia; may cause psychologic problems during emergence	Rapid induction; short procedures when muscle relaxation not needed; children and young adults
Fentanyl	Sublimaze	Intravenous	Opioid; potent narcotic, metabolizes slowly; respiratory depressant	High-dose narcotic anaesthesia in combination with oxygen
Sufentanil citrate	Sufenta	Intravenous	Opioid; potent narcotic, respiratory depressant	Premedication; high-dose narcotic anaesthesia in combination with oxygen
Fentanyl and droperidol	Innovar	Intravenous	Combination narcotic and tranquilizer; potent; long acting	Neuroleptanalgesia
Diazepam	Valium	Intravenous, intramuscular	Benzodiazepine; tranquilizer; produces amnesia, sedation, and muscle relaxation	Premedication; awake intubation; induction
Midazolam	Versed	Intravenous, intramuscular	Benzodiazepine; sedative; short-acting amnesic; central nervous system and respiratory depressant	Premedication; conscious sedation; induction in children

Most Commonly Used General Anaesthetic Agents

An ideal anaesthetic agent or technique suitable for all patients does not exist, but the one selected should include the following characteristics:

- Provides maximum safety for the patient
- Provides optimal operating conditions for the surgeon
- Provides patient comfort
- Has a low index of toxicity
- Provides potent, predictable analgesia extending into the post-operative period
- Produces adequate muscle relaxation
- Provides amnesia
- Has a rapid onset and easy reversibility
- Produces minimum side effects

The following factors are important:

- Age and size/weight of the body
- Physical, mental, and emotional status of the patient
- Presence of complicating systemic disease or concurrent drug therapy
- Presence of infection at the site of the surgical procedure
- Previous anaesthesia experience
- Anticipated procedure
- Position required for the procedure
- Type and expected length of the procedure
- Local or systemic toxicity of the agent
- Expertise of the anaesthesia provider
- Preference of the surgeon and patient.

Anaesthesia Related Drugs

Researchers, technicians and care-persons must have knowledge of the actions, methods of administration, and nursing considerations associated with each drug used in our laboratory. Drugs are commonly placed into categories according to their similarities in action and/or their physiologic effect when introduced into the system. The following two sections describe the basic categories of drugs commonly used in our laboratory. While these two chapters have some detailed descriptions of drugs that are important for our laboratory, they are still useful for the non-specialist, as they explain the specific uses of these drugs in the laboratory, and their dosages for different procedures.

Anticholinergics

Anticholinergic agents may be indicated prior to the administration of a variety of anaesthetic and related agents, including sedatives, narcotics, barbiturates, and inhalant anaesthetic agents. Atropine sulphate, scopolamine, and glycopyrrolate are the three principle anticholinergics used in the laboratory. All three substances are antimuscarinic agents. Muscarinic receptor antagonists prevent the effects of ACh by blocking its binding to muscarinic cholinergic receptors at neuro effector sites on smooth muscle, cardiac muscle, and gland cells; in peripheral ganglia; and in the central nervous system.

Atropine Sulphate

Description: It acts directly on the smooth muscles and secretory glands innervated by postganglionic cholinergic nerves, blocking the para-sympathomimetic effects of acetylcholine. Penetrates the Blood-Brain barrier.

Usage: As a preanaesthetic it is used both because of the mild respiratory stimulation because it inhibits salivary secretion. In reversing paralysis it is used in conjunction with the administration of prostigmin to block the muscarinic receptors. Administration of prostigmin without atropine can cause parasympathetic hyperactivity. Atropine is distributed as such by Elkins-Sinn, Eli Lilly and Astra.

Dosage and Administration: As preanaesthetic — 0.05 mg/kg. To reverse paralysis - 0.15 mg/kg—We usually use the 0.54 mg/ml concentration. For this concentration the dosage for atropine as preanaesthetic is 0.1 ml/kg.

Robinul

Description: Glycopyrrolate, like other anticholinergic (antimuscarinic) agents, inhibits the action of acetylcholine on structures innervated by postganglionic cholinergic nerves and on smooth muscles that respond to acetylcholine but lack cholinergic innervation. These peripheral cholinergic receptors are present in the autonomic effector cells of smooth muscle, cardiac muscle, the sinoatrial node, the atrioventricular node, exocrine glands, and, to a limited degree, in the autonomic ganglia. Thus, it diminishes the volume and free acidity of gastric secretions and controls excessive pharyngeal, tracheal, and bronchial secretions

Usage: In anaesthesia: Robinul (glycopyrrolate) Injectable is indicated for use as a preoperative antimuscarinic to reduce salivary, tracheobronchial, and pharyngeal secretions; to reduce the volume and free acidity of gastric secretions; and, to block cardiac vagal inhibitory reflexes during induction of anaesthesia and intubation.

Dosage and Administration: Robinul (glycopyrrolate) Injectable may be administered intramuscularly, or intravenously, without dilution, in the following indications:

Preanaesthetic medication: The recommended dose of Robinul (glycopyrrolate) — Injectable in children 1 month to 12 years of age is 0.002 mg (0.01 mL) per pound of body weight intramuscularly, given 30 to 60 minutes prior to the anticipated time of induction of anaesthesia or at the time the preanaesthetic narcotic and/or sedative are administered. Children 1 month to 2 years of age may require up to 0.004 mg (0.02 mL) per pound of body weight.

Intraoperative medication: Because of the long duration of action of Robinul (glycopyrrolate) if used as preanaesthetic medication, additional Robinul (glycopyrrolate). Injectable for anticholinergic effect intraoperatively is rarely needed; in the event it is required the recommended pediatric dose is 0.002 mg (0.01 mL) per pound of body weight intravenously, not to exceed 0.1 mg (0.5 mL) in a single dose which may be repeated, as needed, at intervals of 2-3 minutes. The usual attempts should be made to determine the etiology of the arrhythmia, and the surgical or anaesthetic manipulations necessary to correct parasympathetic imbalance should be performed.

Reversal of neuromuscular blockade. The recommended pediatric dose of Robinul (glycopyrrolate) — Injectable is 0.2 mg (1.0 mL) for each 1.0 mg of neostigmine or 5.0 mg of pyridostigmine. In order to minimize the appearance of cardiac side effects, the drugs may be administered simultaneously by intravenous injection and may be mixed in the same syringe.

Anticholinesterases

These agents inhibit acetylcholinesterase (anti-ChE), which is concentrated in synaptic regions and is responsible for the rapid hydrolysis of acetylcholine. Transmitter thus accumulates, and the response to ACh that is liberated by cholinergic impulses or that is spontaneously released from the nerve ending is enhanced. The anticholinesterases reverse the antagonism caused by competitive neuromuscular blocking agents.

Prostigmin (Neostigmine Methylsulphate)

Description: Prostigmin (neostigmine methylsulphate). Injectable, an anticholinesterase agent, is a sterile aqueous solution intended for intramuscular, intravenous or subcutaneous administration. Prostigmin Injectable is available in the following concentrations: Prostigmin 1:2000 Ampoules—each ml contains 0.5 mg neostigmine methylsulphate compounded with 0.2% parabens (methyl and propyl) as preservatives and sodium hydroxide to adjust pH to approximately 5.9.

Usage: For the reversal of effects of nondepolarizing neuromuscular blocking agents.

Dosage and Administration: When Prostigmin is administered intravenously, it is recommended that atropine sulphate (0.6 to 1.2 mg) also be given intravenously using separate syringes. Some authorities have recommended that the atropine be injected several minutes before the Prostigmin rather than concomitantly. The usual dose is 0.5 to 2 mg Prostigmin given by slow intravenous injection, repeated as required. Only in exceptional cases should the total dose of Prostigmin exceed 5 mg. It is recommended that the patient be well ventilated and a patent airway maintained until complete recovery of normal respiration is assured.

Tranquilizers/Anticonvulsants

A number of different drug categories can be used as tranquilizers, including barbiturates and benzodiazepines. Benzodiazepine derivatives are the chlordiazepoxide, diazepam, oxazepam, clorazepate, lorazepam, prazepam, alprazolam, and halazepam. Although commonly used for treating anxiety, these drugs share other therapeutic indications—notably sedation and induction of sleep.

Diazepam (Valium)

Description: Diazepam is a benzodiazepine derivative acting on parts of the limbic system, thalamus and hypothalamus inducing calming effects.

Usage: It can be given as an anticonvulsant, but beware of blood pressure changes. It is distributed as Valium by Roche Products.

Dosage and Administration: 2-5 mg IM or IV.

Phenytoin

Description: Phenytoin is an antiepilectic drug. Dilantin is indicated for the control of tonic-clonic and psychomotor (grand mal and temporal lobe) seizures and prevention and treatment of seizures occurring during or following neurosurgery.

Usage: Diazepam is to be used before phenytoin. It is distributed as Dilantin by Parke-Davis.

Dosage and Administration: 50-100 mg IM 5-10 mg/kg slowly IV.

Phenobarbital

Description: Nonselective CNS depressant of the barbiturate class, that produces drowsiness, sedation, hypnosis, and anticonvulsant effects by depressing sensorimotor activity and cerebellar function. It has a rapid onset of action (about 5 minutes), with peak effects within 30 minutes, and lasts for about 10 hours.

Usage: For depressing seizure activity in animals that may develop an implant infection, or a minor stroke as a result of recording-guide-tube placement. If the monkey is in epileptic status multiply the total amount drug by 3 (*i.e.* 15 mg/kg) and **inject it over 10-15 minutes**. For anticonvulsant therapy administer the total daily amount in 2 doses. Makes antibiotics such as chloramphenicol less effective. If respiratory depression occurs respirate the monkey using our bag-mask resuscitator (Ambu). If depression persist administer doxapram injection.

Dosage and Administration: 0.025 mL/kg/day.

Dissociation Anaesthetics

Some arylcycloalkylamines may induce a state of sedation, immobility, amnesia, and marked analgesia. The name dissociative anaesthesia is derived from the strong feeling of dissociation from the environment that is experienced by the subject to whom such an agent is administered.

Ketamine Hydrochloride (Ketalar)

Description: Ketamine is a non-narcotic, non-barbiturate anaesthetic which produces a dissociative mental state characterized by sedation, amnesia and analgesia. Its pharmacological action is characterized by profound analgesia, normal pharyngeal-laryngeal reflexes.

Effects on CNS: The primary site of CNS action of ketamine appears to be the thalamo-neocortical projection system. It selectively depresses neuronal function in parts of the cortex (especially association areas) and thalamus, while simultaneously stimulating parts of the limbic system, including the hippocampus.

Effects on the Respiratory System: Ketamine has minimal effects on the central respiratory drive as reflected by an unaltered response to carbon dioxide.

Effects on the Cardiovascular System: Ketamine also has unique cardiovascular effects; it stimulates the cardiovascular system and is usually associated with increases in blood pressure, heart rate, and cardiac output.

Usage: Ketamine can be used as a supplement or adjunct to regional anaesthesia, extending the usefulness of the primary (local anesthetic) form of anaesthesia. In this setting ketamine can be used prior to the application of painful blocks, but more commonly it is used for sedation or supplemental anaesthesia during long or uncomfortable procedures. When used for supplementation of regional anaesthesia, ketamine (0.5 mg/kg IV) combined with diazepam (0.15 mg/kg IV) is better accepted by human patients and not associated with greater side effects as compared with unsedated patients.

Dosage and Administration: It can be given IM or IV. It is distributed as Ketalar by Parke-Davis and as Ketaset or Ketaject by Bristol Laboratories. Atropine should be administered beforehand. It causes mild respiratory depression and mild cardiac stimulation. Dosages for different primate species can be found in the following table.

Species	Restraint (mg/kg)	Preanaesthetic (mg/kg)
Aotus trivirgatus (owl)	10-12	20-25 mg/kg
Cebus capuchin	13-15	25-30
Cercopithicus aethiops	10-12	25-30
Macaca fascicullaris	12-15	20-25
M. fuscata (japanese)	5	10
M. mulata (rhesus)	5-10	20-25
M. nemestrina (pig-tail)	5-7.5	15-20
M. radiata (bonnet)	12-15	25-30
M. arctoides (stump-tail)	5-7.5	20-25
Saimiri sciureus (squirrel)	12-15	25-30

Inhalation Anaesthetics

Nitrous Oxide

Description: Nitrous oxide is probably the most common supplement used with opioid-based anaesthesia. Nitrous oxide has minimal effects on cardiovascular dynamics, but still can depress myocardial contractility. In addition, nitrous oxide in combination with opioids is usually associated with significant cardiovascular depression. After administration of morphine (2 mg/kg), nitrous oxide produces concentration-dependent decreases in stroke volume, cardiac output, and arterial blood pressure and increases in SVR.

Usage: For all procedures in which cortical suppression must be avoided. It must always be used together with analgesics.

Dosage and Administration: We typically use this in 1 lt/min with 1 lt/min Oxygen flow (50%).

Isoflurane

Description: Isoflurane is the newest inhalant anaesthetic available. The vapour pressure of isoflurane resembles that of halothane so that it can be administered in a halothane-type vapourizer. Isoflurane has the largest circulatory margin of safety of all potent halogenated agents. It produces the least myocardial depression at a given multiple of the minimum alveolar concentration.

Usage: We use it for all surgical procedures requiring general surgical anaesthesia.

Dosage and Administration: We typically use 3.5% for a 6 to 8 kg animal for about 3 minutes, and subsequently reduce the concentration to 1.2-1.5%. Isoflurane is metabolized to such a small extent that any increase in metabolism would be inconsequential. There is greater protection of the liver during isoflurane anaesthesia than halothane. Finally, in sharp contrast to halothane, isoflurane is nonflammable.

Desflurane

Description: Desflurane (SUPRANE) is the newest volatile anaesthetic and has low solubility in lipids and blood. Chemically it is the difluoromethyl 1-fluoro-2,2,2-trifluoroethyl ether.

Usage: We use it for procedures that require immediate waking up of the animal.

Dosage and Administration: 4-6% with air or 3% with N_2O.

Intravenous Barbiturate Anaesthetics

The barbiturates reversibly depress the activity of all excitable tissues. The CNS is exquisitely sensitive, and, even when barbiturates are given in anaesthetic concentrations, direct effects on peripheral excitable tissues are weak. However, serious deficits in cardiovascular and other peripheral functions occur in acute barbiturate intoxication.

Pentobarbital

Description: Pentobarbital is a barbiturate anaesthetic, supplied as Nembutal by Abbott Laboratories. It is used to provide anaesthesia for long surgical procedures. Its duration of action ranges from 30-60 minutes. There is a tendency to underdose small animals and overdose large animals in the same species and age group because drug doses within a group ultimately depend on metabolic size. This is the anaesthetic most commonly used in this laboratory.

Usage: Rarely for general anaesthesia.

Dosage and Administration: Nembutal 24-30 mg/kg, but when ketamine or other preanaesthetic on board, use about 1/3 to 1/6 of it, so either 8 mg/kg or 4 mg/kg. Induction dose depends on the drugs used to restrain the animal on.

Thiopental

Description: Thiopental is an ultra-short-acting thio-barbiturate used for induction of anaesthesia. It is distributed as Pentothal by Abbott Laboratories.

Respiration: Unlike some of the inhalational anaesthetics, thiopental.

Usage: For single-unit recordings is the only appropriate barbiturate since pentobarbital suppresses cell activity.

Dosage and Administration: A total 15-20 mg/kg IV should be given to effect (at 30 sec. intervals) start with a third to a half of the calculated dosage is not irritating to the respiratory tract, and yet coughing, laryngospasm, and even bronchospasm occur with some frequency.

Intravenous Nonbarbiturate Anaesthetics

Diprivan Injection (Propofol)

Description: Diprivan Injection is an intravenous sedative hypnotic agent for use in the induction and maintenance of anaesthesia or sedation.

Usage: Diprivan Injection is an IV anesthetic agent that can be used for both induction and/or maintenance of anaesthesia as part of a balanced anesthetic technique for inpatient and outpatient surgery in adults and in children 3 years of age or older.

Induction of General Anaesthesia: Monkeys require 2.5 to 3.5 mg/kg of Diprivan Injection for induction when unpremedicated or when lightly premedicated with oral benzodiazepines or intramuscular opioids. As with other sedative hypnotic agents, the amount of intravenous opioid and/or benzodiazepine premedication will influence the response of the patient to an induction dose of Diprivan Injection. Attention should be paid to minimize pain on injection when administering Diprivan Injection to animals. Rapid boluses of Diprivan Injection may be administered if small veins are pretreated with lidocaine or when antecubital or larger veins are utilized. Diprivan Injection administered in a variable rate infusion with nitrous oxide 60-70% provides satisfactory anaesthesia for most pediatric patients 3 years of age or older, ASA I or II, undergoing general anaesthesia.

Maintenance of General Anaesthesia: Maintenance by infusion of Diprivan Injection at a rate of 200-300 mcgm/kg/min should immediately follow the induction dose. Following the first half hour of maintenance, if clinical signs of light anaesthesia are not present, the infusion rate should be decreased; during this period, infusion rates of 125-150 mcgm/kg/min are typically needed. However, younger children (5 years or less) may require larger maintenance infusion rates than older children.

Dosage and Administration: Induction dose for monkeys: 2.5 to 3.5 mg/kg administered over 20-30 seconds. Infusion for monkeys: 125 to 300 mcgm/kg/min (7.5 to 18 mg/kg/h). When indicated, initiation of sedation should begin at 5 mcgm/kg/min (0.3 mg/kg/h). The infusion rate should be increased by increments of 5 to 10 mcgm/kg/min (0.3 to 0.6 mg/kg/h) until the desired level of sedation is achieved. A minimum period of 5 minutes between adjustments should be allowed for onset of peak drug effect. Bolus administration of 10 or 20 mg should only be used to rapidly increase depth of sedation in patients where hypotension is not likely to occur.

Dilution Prior to Administration: When Diprivan Injection is diluted prior to administration, it should only be diluted with 5% Dextrose Injection, USP, and it should not be diluted to a concentration less than 2 mg/mL because it is an emulsion. In diluted form it has been shown to be more stable when in contact with glass than with plastic (95% potency after 2 hours of running infusion in plastic).

Administration with other fluids: Compatibility of Diprivan Injection with the coadministration of blood/serum/plasma has not been established. Diprivan Injection has been shown to be compatible when administered with the following intravenous fluid.

Xylazine

Description: Xylazine is a non-narcotic compound acting as sedative and analgesic as well as a muscle relaxant. Xylazine is distributed as Rompun by Bayvet Division of Miles Laboratories. The principal pharmacological activities develop 3 to 5 min after IV and 10 to 15 min after IM injection. Its major usefulness, however, is when combined with ketamine. Always premedicate with atropine. Xylazine can cause vomiting.

Usage: We mainly use it in combination with Ketamine for minor procedures, which however require the avoidance of unwanted animal-movements.

Dosage and Administration: Dosage 0.5-1.0 mg/kg IM. The combination of ketamine and xylazine provides effect anaesthesia for moderate duration procedures. The two substances can be delivered from the same syringe. Dosage 0.6 mg/kg xylazine and 7 mg/kg ketamine.

Local Anaesthetics

Local anaesthetics prevent the generation and the conduction of the nerve impulse. Their primary site of action is the cell membrane. Conduction block can be demonstrated in squid giant axons from which the axoplasm has been removed. Local anaesthetics block conduction by decreasing or preventing the large transient increase in the permeability of excitable membranes to Na^+ that normally is produced by a slight depolarization of the membrane. This action of local anaesthetics is due to their direct interaction with voltage-gated Na^+ channels. As the anesthetic action progressively develops in a nerve, the threshold for electrical excitability gradually increases, the rate of rise of the action potential declines, impulse conduction slows, and the safety factor for conduction decreases; these factors decrease the probability of propagation of the action potential, and nerve conduction fails.

Lidocaine

Lidocaine is used to produce local anaesthesia following subcutaneous injection. It is distributed as Xylocaine by Astra and as Lidocaine by Elkins-Sinn. Dosage 0.5% solution for infiltration anaesthesia.

Procaine

Procaine is a synthetic local anaesthetic. It is readily absorbed following parenteral administration and thus does not long remain at the site of injection. It is supplied as Novocaine by Winthrop–Breon. Dosage 0.25-0.5% for infiltration anaesthesia, 0.5-2.0% for peripheral nerve block, and 10% for spinal anaesthesia.

Muscle Relaxants

Vecuronium bromide

Description: Norcuron (vecuronium bromide) for injection is a nondepolarizing neuromuscular blocking agent of intermediate duration. Norcuron is supplied as a sterile nonpyrogenic freeze-dried buffered cake of very fine microscopic crystalline particles for intravenous injection only. Each 10 mL vial contains 10 mg vecuronium bromide, 20.75 mg citric acid anhydrous, 16.25 mg sodium phosphate dibasic anhydrous, 97 mg mannitol (to adjust tonicity), sodium hydroxide and/or phosphoric acid to buffer and adjust to a pH of 4. Each 20 mL vial contains 20 mg of vecuronium bromide, 41.5 mg citric acid anhydrous, 32.5 mg sodium phosphate dibasic anhydrous, 194 mg mannitol (to adjust tonicity), sodium hydroxide and/or phosphoric acid to buffer and adjust to a pH of 4.

Usage: Used for muscle relations in neurophysiology experiments and some of the MRI experiments.

Dosage and Administration: Norcuron (vecuronium bromide) for injection is for intravenous use only. To obtain maximum clinical benefits of Norcuron and to minimize the possibility of overdosage, the monitoring of muscle twitch response to peripheral nerve stimulation is advised. The recommended initial dose of **Norcuron is 0.08 to 0.10 mg/kg (1.4 to 1.75 times the ED90)** given as an intravenous bolus injection. This dose can be expected to produce good or excellent non-emergency intubation conditions in 2.5 to 3 minutes after injection. Under balanced anaesthesia, clinically required neuromuscular blockade lasts approximately 25-30 minutes, with recovery to 25% of control achieved approximately 25 to 40 minutes after injection and recovery to 95% of control achieved approximately 45-65 minutes after injection. In the presence of potent inhalation anesthetics, the neuromuscular blocking effect of Norcuron is enhanced. If Norcuron is first administered more than 5 minutes after the start of inhalation agent or when steady-state has been achieved, the initial Norcuron dose may be reduced by **approximately 15%, *i.e.*, 0.060 to 0.085 mg/kg.**

Fentanyl

Description: Fentanyl is an opioid analgesic. Fentanyl interacts predominately with the opioid mu-receptor. These mu-binding sites are discretely distributed in the human brain, spinal cord, and other tissues. In clinical settings, fentanyl exerts its principal pharmacologic effects on the central nervous system. Its primary actions of therapeutic value are analgesia and sedation. Fentanyl may increase the patient's tolerance for pain and decrease the perception of suffering, although the presence of the pain itself may still be recognized.

Usage: Used in surgical procedure as perioperative analgesic.

Dosage and Administration: Fentanyl is 100 times more potent than morphine. The onset of the drug is immediate when it is given IV and the duration of action is 30 to 60 min after a single IV dose of 100 micrograms. Following IM injection the onset is 7 to 8 min and the duration is 1 to 2 hr. It is distributed as Sublimaze by Janssen Pharmaceutica. Dosage 0.05-0.15 milligram / kg IM or SQ.

Sufentanil

Sufentanil, which is 7 to 10 times as potent as fentanyl, causes hypotension with equal or greater frequency as compared with the latter. Since sufentanil is available in concentrations similar to those of fentanyl (50 mg/ml) one obvious possible cause of hypotension is relative overdose. Sufentanil does not produce increases in plasma histamine but does cause vagal-induced bradycardia. As with fentanyl, mild to no depression of cardiac index and pump function is usually observed after sufentanil in humans. Ablation of sympathetic tone and enhanced parasympathetic tone are the most likely mechanisms for sufentanil-associated hypotension. Sufentanil-induced hypotension may also be mediated by a direct depression of vascular smooth muscle.

Several studies suggest that sufentanil not only is more potent than fentanyl but also is closer to a "complete anesthetic." These claims are supported by greater MAC reduction during coadministration of inhalation anaesthetics in laboratory animals and less hemodynamic responses to stimuli such as intubation in humans 180 as compared with fentanyl. Sufentanil can cause more hypotension than equipotent doses of fentanyl. It is found that sufentanil (5 mg/kg) produces lower mean arterial blood pressures than fentanyl (25 mg/kg) during induction of anaesthesia in patients undergoing coronary artery surgery. It has been also shown that although sufentanil (15 mg/kg) attenuated the hemodynamic response to endotracheal intubation better than fentanyl (75 mg/kg), it impaired myocardial function and depressed systolic blood pressure more.

Usage: Analgesic used during and after surgical procedures.

Naloxone

Description: Narcan, a narcotic antagonist, is a synthetic congener of oxymorphone. It antagonizes the opioid effects by competing for the same receptor sites. Thus, reversing narcotic depression resulting from opioid overdose. Its duration of action is approximately 4 hours; therefore, it may need to be administered more than once. It is distributed as Narcan by Du Pont. When using Narcan against Buprenex you may need to use 10X the normal dose.

Usage: To reverse the effects of possible overdose of narcotics. Note that Naloxone is not effective against respiratory depression due to non-opioid drugs. Reversal of buprenorphine-induced respiratory depression may be incomplete. If an incomplete response occurs, respirations should be mechanically assisted using AMBU.

Dosage and Administration: Dosage 0.01-0.05 mg/kg IM or IV. We usually use the 0.4 mg/kg concentration. For this concentration and for an average "dosage" of 0.03 mg/kg the dosage is: 0.075 ml/kg.

Non-Opioid Analgesics

Acetaminophen

Description: Distributed as Tylenol. Given prior to and following surgery for 48 hours, often in conjunction with other analgesics. Provides mild to moderate analgesia. Can be found in variety of size tablets. Often it is convenient to use children's Tylenol because of the smaller number of milligrams per tablet. Tylenol can be also found in a syrup form.

Usage: For mild analgesia.

Dosage and Administration: 10 mg/kg P.O. 2 times daily.

Bacitracinneomycinpolymyxin

Description: Commonly referred to as "triple antibiotic", this ointment is for external use only. Do not apply to the eye.

Usage: We use this around the headpost after it has been cleaned and postoperatively on the surgical wounds to prevent infections.

Dosage and Administration: Apply as needed directly upon the infected area. Usually once a day.

Cephalothin

Description: Cephalothin is a broad-spectrum antibiotic acting against *Streptococci, Staphylococci, Klebsiella, Salmonella*. It should be reserved for serious infections.

Usage: Drs. Neil Lipman and Robert Marini, the veterinarians at MIT, suggested this drug strongly for meningitis. It should be used with caution, as it is as dangerous as the chloramphenicol. It is distributed as Keflin by Eli Lilly and as Seffin by Glaxo. In ointment it can be also used for the eye, if a corneal ulcer is present. In the latter case do not use a steroid-based ophthalmic solution or ointment. If in doubt, get veterinarian to examine eye. Do not confuse Cephalothin with the regular triple antibiotics (that cannot be applied on the eye).

Dosage and Administration: The ointment can be applied to the eye 3-4 times daily. Dosage 20-35 mg/kg IV, IM, SQ, two or three times per day. We usually use Keflin (100 mg/ml). For this concentration the dosage during surgery is 0.30 ml/kg Bacitracin-neomycin-polymyxin-hydrocortisone.

Erythromycin

Description: Erythromycin is mainly an orally effective antibiotic, and the IV injection is indicated only when oral administration is impossible. It does not penetrate the blood-brain barrier, but it diffuses readily into intracellular fluids, and antibacterial activity can be achieved at essentially all the other sites. It can be used for minor *streptococcal* and *staphylococcal* infections.

Usage: Used in the chambers or systemically, according to the veterinarian's instructions.

Dosage and Administration: Erythromycin lactobionate 10-20 mg/kg I.V. per day. It must be administered by continuous infusion. Erythromycin ethylsuccinate suspensions may be administered without regard to meals in a dosage 10-20 mg/kg/day in equally divided doses. For severe infections this dosage may be doubled.

Neosporin Ophthalmic Ointment

Description: Neosporin Ophthalmic Ointment (neomycin and polymyxin B sulphates and bacitracin zinc ophthalmic ointment) is a sterile antimicrobial ointment for ophthalmic use.

Usage: A wide range of antibacterial action is provided by the overlapping spectra of neomycin, polymyxin B sulphate, and bacitracin. Neomycin is bactericidal for many gram-positive and gram-negative organis.

Dosage and Administration: Apply the ointment every 3 or 4 hours for 7 to 10 days, depending on the severity of the infection.

Adrenergic Drugs

Epinephrine

Description: Epinephrine is a sympathomimetic drug. It is the most potent alpha receptor activator. It is given as an emergency dose for failing circulation or extremely congested respiration. It is not used in cardiac failure or in hemorrhagic, traumatic, or cariogenic shock. It is also used as hemostatic agent.

Adrenergic Drugs

Epinephrine

Description: Epinephrine is a sympathomimetic drug. It is the most potent alpha receptor activator. It is given as an emergency dose for failing circulation or extremely congested respiration. It is not used in cardiac failure or in hemorrhagic, traumatic, or cariogenic shock. It is also used as hemostatic agent.

Usage: Epinephrine is used in cardiac asystole or in cases where a pressor effect is needed immediately to counter decreases in blood pressure. Phenylephrine can also be used to elevate blood pressure. It is distributed as Adrenaline injection by Parke-Davis and as Epinephrine injection by Astra, Elkins-Sinn and Astra. We generally use it with saline irrigation fluid, since it constricts blood vessels and therefore decreases bleeding.

Dosage and Administration: 0.01 mg/kg IV or IM for irrigation: 1 ml/200ml saline.

1. **Dextrose**
   1. Dextrose (5%) Injection, USP
   2. Dextrose (5%) in Lactated Ringer's Injection

3. Dextrose (5%) in Ringer's Injection

4. Dextrose (5%) and Sodium Chloride (0.45%) Injection, USP

5. Dextrose (5%) and Sodium Chloride (0.9%) Injection, USP

2. **Concentration of Lactated Ringer**

1. Lactated Ringer's Injection, USP

2. Potassium Chloride (40 mEq /liter) in Dextrose (5%) Injection, USP

3. Sodium Chloride (0.45%) Injection, USP

4. Sodium Chloride (0.9%) Injection, USP

5. Brevibloc injection **is not compatible** with Sodium Bicarbonate (5%) Injection, USP

Anti-inflammatory Agents

Decadron (Dexamethasone)

Description: Decadron (Dexamethasone sodium phosphate), a synthetic adrenocortical steroid, is a white or slightly yellow, crystalline powder. It is freely soluble in water and is exceedingly hygroscopic. Each milliliter of decadron Phosphate injection, 4 mg/mL, contains dexamethasone sodium phosphate equivalent to 4 mg dexamethasone phosphate or 3.33 mg dexamethasone.

Usage: Preoperatively, and in the event of serious trauma or illness, in patients with known adrenal insufficiency or when adrenocortical reserve is doubtful. Shock unresponsive to conventional therapy if adrenocortical insufficiency exists or is suspected.

Dosage and Administration: Decadron Phosphate injection, 4 mg/mL—For intravenous, intramuscular, intra-articular, intralesional, and soft tissue injection. Decadron phosphate injection, 24 mg/mL—For intravenous injection only.

Solu-Medrol (Methylprednisolone)

Description: Solu-Medrol Sterile Powder contains methylprednisolone sodium succinate as the active ingredient. Methylprednisolone sodium succinate, USP, occurs as a white, or nearly white, odorless hygroscopic, amorphous solid. It is very soluble in water and in alcohol; it is insoluble in chloroform and is very slightly soluble in acetone. Naturally occurring glucocorticoids (hydrocortisone and cortisone), which also have salt-retaining properties, are used as replacement therapy in adrenocortical deficiency states.

Usage: In cases of brain injury due to electrodes or to implanted guide tubes. Note that convulsions have been reported with concurrent use of methylprednisolone and cyclosporin. Drugs that induce hepatic enzymes such as phenobarbital, phenytoin and rifampin may increase the clearance of methylprednisolone and may require increases in methylprednisolone dose to achieve the desired response. Drugs such as troleandomycin and ketoconazole may inhibit the metabolism of methylprednisolone and thus decrease its clearance.

Dosage and Administration: When high dose therapy is desired, the recommended dose of Solu-Medrol Sterile Powder is 30 mg/kg administered intravenously over at least 30 minutes. This dose may be repeated every 4 to 6 hours for 48 hours. In general, high dose corticosteroid therapy should be continued only until the patient's condition has stabilized; usually not beyond 48 to 72 hours. Although adverse effects associated with high dose short-term corticoid therapy are uncommon, peptic ulceration may occur. Prophylactic antacid therapy may be indicated. In other indications initial dosage will vary from 10 to 40 mg of methylprednisolone depending on the clinical problem being treated. The larger doses may be required for short-term management of severe, acute conditions.

Anticoagulants

Heparin

Description: Heparin Sodium Injection, USP is a sterile solution of heparin sodium derived from bovine lung tissue, standardized for anticoagulant activity. Heparin is a heterogeneous group of straight-chain anionic mucopolysaccharides called glycosaminoglycans having anticoagulant properties.

Usage: We use it in sterile saline to flush IV catheters. We also use it in the rinse solution for a perfusion.

Dosage and Administration: Dosage is 2 units/ml saline. We usually use the 1,000 units/ml concentration. For this concentration the dosage is 0.5 ml/(250 ml saline [0.9% sodium chloride]). Heparin is to be administered IV or by deep subcutaneous routes.

Protamine

Description: Protamines are simple proteins of low molecular weight, rich in arginine and strongly basic. This strongly basic nature accounts for their antiheparin effect which makes it a useful antidote to heparin overdose. It is distributed as such by Eli Lilly.

Usage: In cases of Heparin Overdose (Should never happen!)

Dosage and Administration: It should be given IV very slowly; not more than 50 mg in every 10-minute period. Each mg protamine neutralizes 90 USP units of heparin.

Diuretics

Furosemide

Description: Furosemide is a potent diuretic which is effective 5-10 minutes after IV administration.

Usage: We use it for the control of intracranial pressure. It is distributed as Lasix by Hoechst-Roussel.

Dosage and Administration: 2-8 mg/kg IV.

Drug Dosage Charts for MPIK Minimum Alveolar Concentration

Drugs Dosage Duration

Anticholinergics

Atropine	0.02-0.05 mg/kg IM
Glycopyrrolate	0.005-0.01 mg/kg IM

Dissociatives

Ketamine	5-20 mg/kg IM 15-30 min
Ketamine & xylazine	7 mg/kg & 0.6 mg/kg IM 15-30 min
Ketamine & xylazine	10 mg/kg & 0.25-2 mg/kg IM 45-138 min
Tiletamine & zolazepam	1.5-3.0 mg/kg IM & 4-6 mg/kg IM 45-60 min

Barbiturate Anesthetics

Pentobarbital	20-30 mg/kg IV (induction) 30-60 min
Pentobarbital	8 mg/kg I f 15 mg/kg Ketamine used
Thiopental	5-7 mg/kg IV (induction)

Non-barbiturate Anesthetics

Propofol	2.5-5 mg/kg IV (induction) 5-10 min
Propofol	0.3-0.4 mg/kg/min (infusion)

Neuroleptanalgesics

Fentanyl-droperidol (Innovar-Vet)	0.1-0.3 ml/kg IM
Fentanyl-fluanisone (Hypnorm)	0.3 ml/kg IM

Opioid Analgesics

Fentanyl	0.003 mg/kg IV 15 min
Sufenta	0.01 mg/kg
Sufenta mite	0.01 mg/kg
Morphine	1-2 mg/kg IM 4 hr
Oxymorphone	0.15 mg/kg IM 4-6 hr
Meperidine	2 mg/kg IM 4 hr
Buprenophrine	0.01 mg/kg IM 6-8 hr

Non-Opioid Analgesics

Aspirin	325 mg PO
Aspiring rectal suppositories	125 mg/5kg
Ketorolac	15-30 mg IM

Drugs Dosage Duration

Muscle Relaxants

Pancuronium	0.08-0.1 mg/kg IV followed by 03 ug/kg/min
Vecuronium	0.04-0.06 mg/kg IV followed by 0.4 ug/kg/min
Atracurium	0.25-0.3 mg/kg IV followed by 1.5 ug/kg/min

Anticholinesterases

Neostigmine	0.05 mg/kg

Miscellaneous

Valium   5 mg
Brevibloc   0.05 mg/kg
Dopram   5 mg/kg
Naloxon   0.04 mg/kg

Temperature

Monitoring is now required (previously recommended).

Sites

- Pulmonary artery = "Core" temperature (gold standard).
- Tympanic membrane-correlates well with core; approximates brain/ hypothalamic temperature.
- Esophagus-correlates well with core.
- Nasopharyngeal-correlates well with core and brain temperature.
- Rectal-not accurate (temp affected by LE venous return, enteric organisms, and stool insulation).
- Bladder-approximates core when urine flow is high.
- Axillary-inaccurate; varies by skin perfusion.
- Skin-inaccurate; varies by site.
- Oropharynx-good estimate of core temperature; recent studies show correlation with tympanic and esophageal temperatures.

Crystalloids

Colloids

Hetastarch (6% hydroxyethyl starch, HES)

- Hespan (in NS) and Hextend (in LR) solutions.
- Solution of highly branched glucose chains (average MW 450 kD).
- Degraded by amylase, eliminated by kidney.
- Intravascular $t_{1/2}$ = 25.5 hrs; tissue $t_{1/2}$ = 10-15 days.
- Maximum Dose: 15-20 ml/kg/day.
- Side effects:
  - Can increase PTT (via factor VIII/ vWF inhibition) and clotting times.
  - Anaphylactoid reactions with wheezing and urticaria may occur.
  - May interfere with platelet function.
- Contraindications: coagulopathy, heart failure, renal failure.

Albumin (5% and 25%)

- Derived from pooled donated blood after cold ethanol extraction and ultra-filtration; heat-treated (60 degree C × 10 hrs).
- Use 5% for hypovolemia; 25% for hypovolemia in patients with restricted fluid and Na intake.
- Minimal risk for viral infection (hepatitis or HIV); theoretical risk of prion transmission.

Crystalloid or Colloid?

Advantages **Disadvantages**

Crystalloid

- Lower cost
- Readily available
  1. Requires more volume for the same hemodynamic effect
  2. Short IV $t_{1/2}$ (20-30 min)
  3. Dilutes plasma proteins
- Peripheral/pulmonary edema
  4. May cause coagulopathy

Colloid

- Restores IV volume and HD with less volume, less time
- Longer IV $t_{1/2}$
- Maintains plasma oncotic pressure
- Less cerebral edema (in healthy brain tissue)
- Less intestinal edema

Disadvantage

1. Expensive
- Coagulopathy (dextran > HES)
  2. Limited by max dose
  3. Potential renal complications
  4. May cause cerebral edema (in areas of injured brain)

Burns

- Increased evaporative losses.
- H_2O, electrolytes, and protein shift from normal to burned tissue, causing intravascular hypovolemia.
- Volume to infuse is calculated by the Parkland Formula.

Parkland Formula

- Volume = % BSA × 4 ml/kg × kg
- Give 1/2 over the 1st 8 hours.
- Give 1/2 over the next 16 hours.
- Replace with LR.
- % BSA is determined by the
- Rule of Nines

Packed Red Blood Cells Indications (ASA Guidelines)

1. Hg < 6 in young, healthy patients
2. Usually unnecessary when Hg >10
3. At Hgb 6-10 g/dl, the decision to transfuse is based on:
1. ongoing indications of organ ischemia
2. potential or ongoing blood loss
3. volume status
4. risk factors for complications of inadequate O_2.

Note: Solutions incompatible with pRBC: LR (theoretical clot formation due to calcium)

D5W, hypotonic solutions (less than 0.9% saline – hemolysis)

- "Blood pumps" use Normal Saline for this reason.

Platelets

Definition, Use and Storage

- Platelet Concentrate (PC)
  - Platelets from one donated unit, vol = 50-70 ml; — plt ~5000-10,000.
  - "6-pack" = 6 pooled PCs; rarely used anymore
- Apheresis Unit
  - Platelets from a single donor; vol = 200-400 ml; plt ~50,000.
- Can give ABO-incompatible platelets, Rh tested only
- Stored at room temperature for — 5 days.
- Hang separately — not through fluid warmer, level 1, or Belmont

Indications (ASA Guidelines)

1. Rarely when plt > 100,000.
2. Usually when plt < 50,000 (spontaneous bleed at < 20K).
3. When plt 50-100,000, based on risk of bleeding.
4. With platelet dysfunction (e.g. CPB, plt inhibitors.

Hypokalemia

Definition

- Mild K+ = 3.1-3.5 mEq/L

- Moderate K + > 3 mEq/L with PACs
- Severe K + < 3 mEq/L with PVCs

Contributing Factors

Pre-operative

- GI losses (NGT, N/V, Diarrhea)
- Lasix, RTA
- Magnesium deficiency

Intra-operative

- Alkalosis (both metabolic and respiratory)
- Insulin therapy
- Hypothermia

Hypokalemia

Signs & Symptoms

- Acute hypokalemia causes hyperpolarization of the cardiac cell and may lead to ventricular escape activity, re-entrant phenomena, ectopic tachycardias, and delayed conduction.
- Arrhythmias
  - PACs, PVCs
  - SVTs (esp. A Fib/A flutter)
- Metabolic alkalosis
- Autonomic lability
- Weakness, — DTRs
- Ileus
- Digoxin toxicity
- Enhanced response to muscle relaxants.

NPO Guidelines

- There is no evidence for the routine use of metoclopramide, H_2– blockers, proton pump inhibitors, antiemetics, or anticholinergics in preventing aspiration or in reducing its morbidity/mortality.
- If given preoperatively, only nonparticulate antacids (Sodium).

Ingested Material Minimum Fasting Period

Clears	2 hours
Breast Milk	4 hours
Formula	6 hours
Non-human Milk	6 hours
Light Meal	6 hours
Fatty Meal	6-8 hours

Orthopaedic Cast Application

Above Elbow Backslab (Adult)

Indications

- Acute distal radius and ulna fractures greater than 2.5 cm from epiphysis of the radius.
- Clinical fractures of elbow, hand, wrist or forearm.
- Forearm and elbow fractures
- Refer to Treatment Profiles for relevant diagnostic tests.

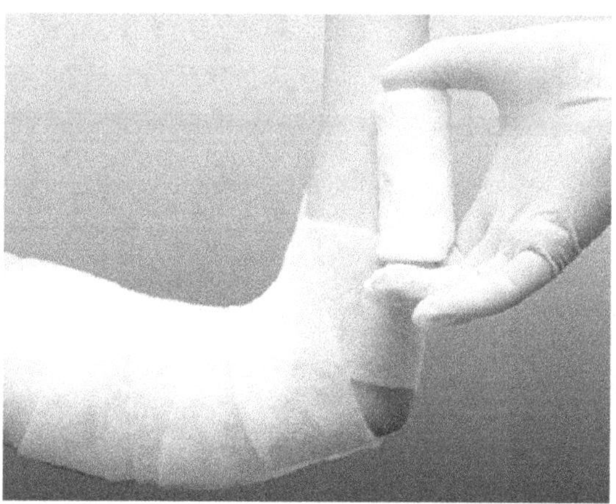

Fig. 1.

Function

- Immobilise elbow and wrist allowing full movement of fingers.

Position

- Wrist in neutral, limb held by assistant with elbow at 90°.

- Proximal limit – axilla, leaving shoulder free
- Distal limit – proximal palmar

Materials

- Double thickness 15-20 cm slab POP.
- 2 × 10 cm slab for struts

Application

- Apply double layer cast padding from proximal palmar crease to axilla, ensuring no edges in elbow crease
- Measure slab from palmar crease to 2 cm distal to axilla
- Wet slab; apply from palmar crease to axilla covering 50% of dorsal and ventral surfaces of wrist, forearm and upper arm along ulnar border of limb
- Wet 10 cm slabs; apply struts to elbows as shown in diagram
- Turn back padding
- Apply bandage firmly
- Put arm in broad arm sling for forearm fractures or a collar and cuff for elbow injuries.

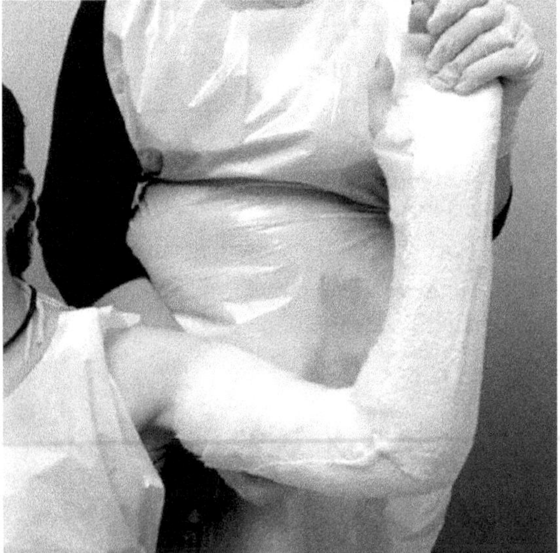

Fig. 2.

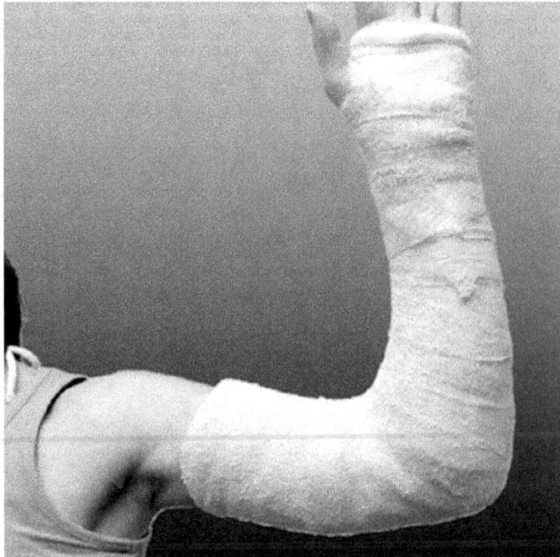

Fig. 4.

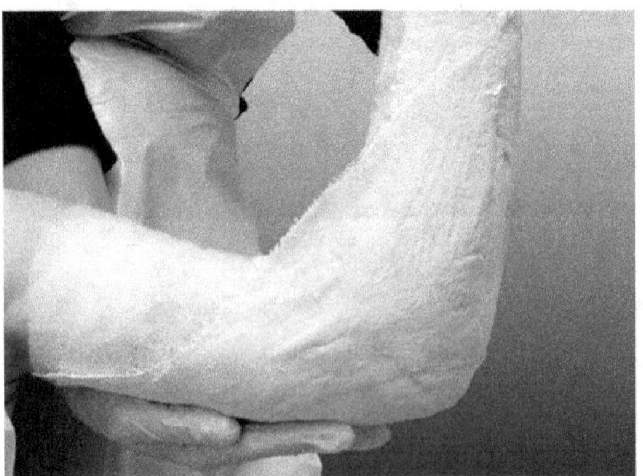

Fig. 3.

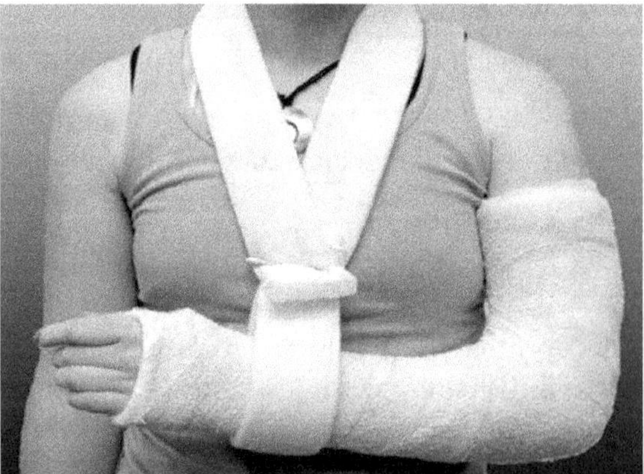

Fig. 5.

Below Elbow Backslab (Adult)

Indications

- Acute distal radius and ulna fractures less than 2.5 cm from epiphysis of the radius
- Severe soft tissue injuries of wrist or forearm
- Clinical factures of wrist or forearm
- Refer to Treatment Profiles for relevant diagnostic tests.

Function

- To provide immobilisation allowing movement of fingers and elbow and to allow rotation of forearm.

Position

- Wrist in neutral
- Proximal limit — 4 cm distal to elbow crease
- Distal limit — proximal palmar crease.

Materials

- Stockinet
- Cast padding
- POP slab double thickness
- Bandage and sling.

Application

- Apply stockinet to forearm
- Cut hole for thumb
- Apply single layer of padding from proximal palmar crease to 4 cm distal to elbow crease with double layer over bony prominences
- Cut slab to shape
- Check slab length on arm extending from proximal palmar crease to 4 cm from elbow crease
- Dip slab in water holding both ends and squeeze gently maintaining shape
- Lay on dorsal aspect of forearm ensuring MCP joints are visible and there is a gap along ventral surface
- Turn back stockinet
- Apply wet bandage
- Apply sling

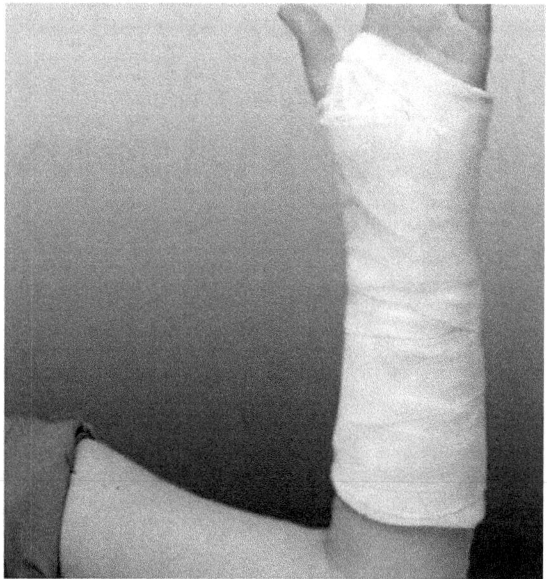

Fig. 6.   **Fig. 7.**

Below Elbow Complete Cast (Adult)

Indications

- Non-acute distal radius and ulna fractures less than 2.5 cm proximal to the distal radial epiphysis.
- Refer to Treatment Profiles for relevant diagnostic tests.

Contra-indications

- Acute injuries or gross swelling

Function

- Immobilise wrist
- Allow full movement of MCPs and Elbow.

Application

- Apply stockinet to forearm
- Cut hole for thumb
- Apply single layer of padding from palmar crease to 4 cm distal to elbow crease with double layer over bony prominences
- Cut double layer POP slab to reinforce the ulnar border and a hand piece split for thumb web space
- Apply wet POP slabs as shown
- Turn over edges of stockinette/padding
- Complete cast with roll of POP
- Mould well while POP setting
- Leave cast with smooth finish.

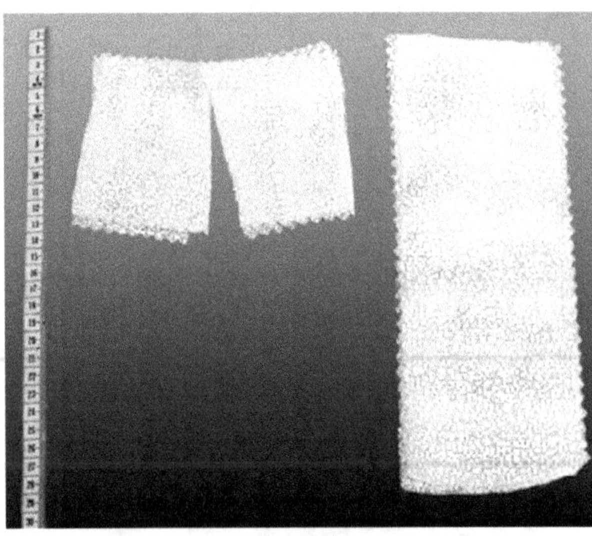

Fig. 8

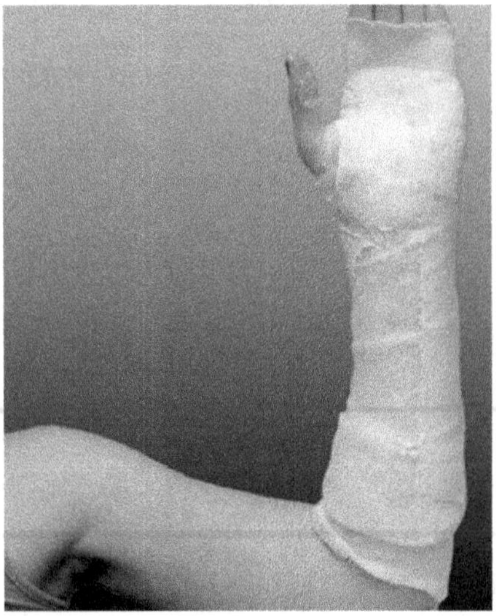

Fig. 9

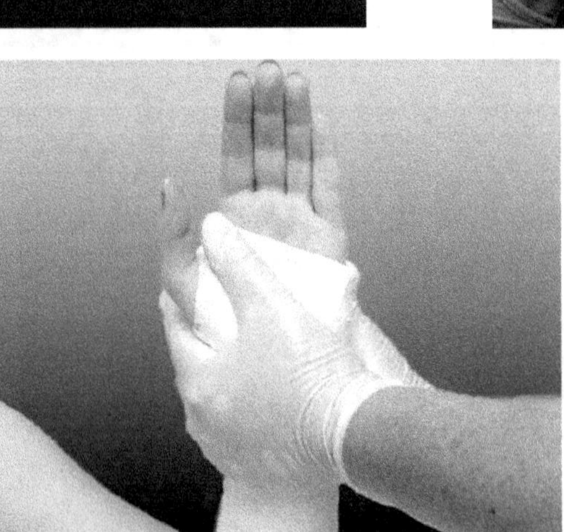

Fig. 10

Above Elbow Complete Cast (Adult)

Indications

- Post-acute radius and ulna fractures more than 2.5 cm proximal to distal radial epiphysis
- Non-acute forearm and elbow fractures
- Refer to Treatment Profiles for relevant diagnostic tests.

Contra-indications

- Acute fractures
- Swelling of wrist, forearm or elbow.

Position

- Forearm in neutral/pronation/supination
- Limb held by assistant
- Elbow at 90°
- Proximal limit – axilla, leaving shoulder free
- Distal limit – proximal palmar crease.

Materials

- Stockinet
- Cast padding
- POP slabs as shown
- 2-3 rolls 7.5-10 cm POP.

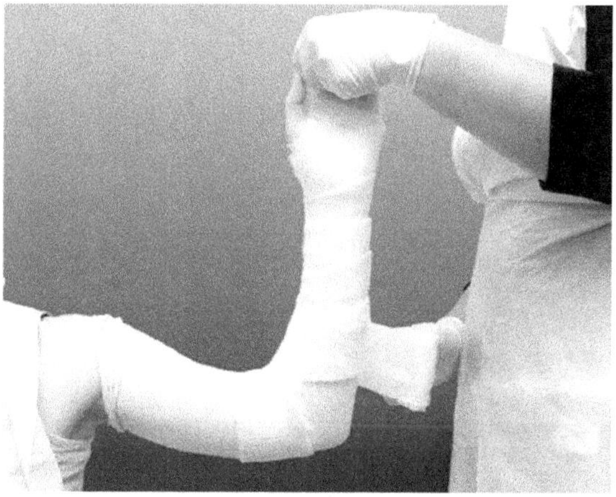

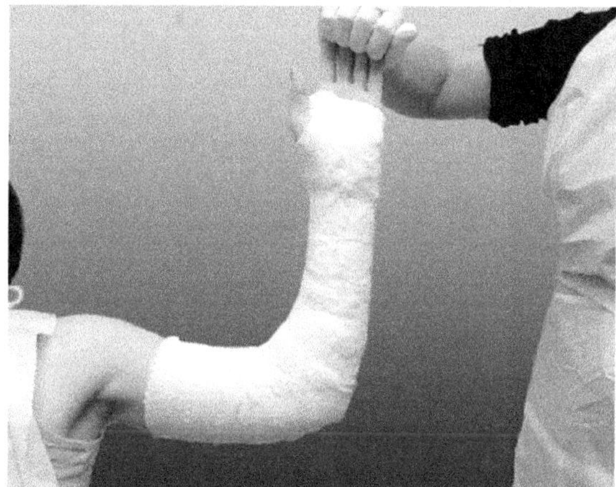

Fig. 11.

Fig. 12.

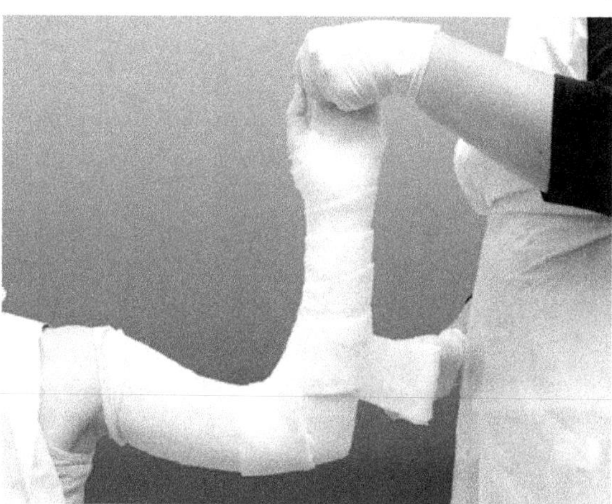

Fig. 13.

Below Knee Complete Cast (Adult)

Indications

- Post-acute fractures of ankle and foot
- Refer to Treatment Profiles for relevant diagnostic tests.

Contra-indications

- Swelling of ankle and foot
- Acute injury (use below knee back slab.

Position

- Ankle at 90°
- Proximal limit – tibial tuberosity, and 1 cm below (distal to) fibular head to avoid damage to common peroneal nerve
- Distal limit – web of toes.

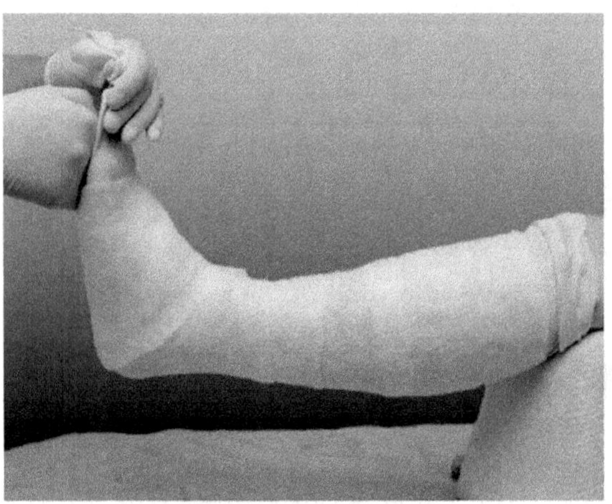

Fig. 14.

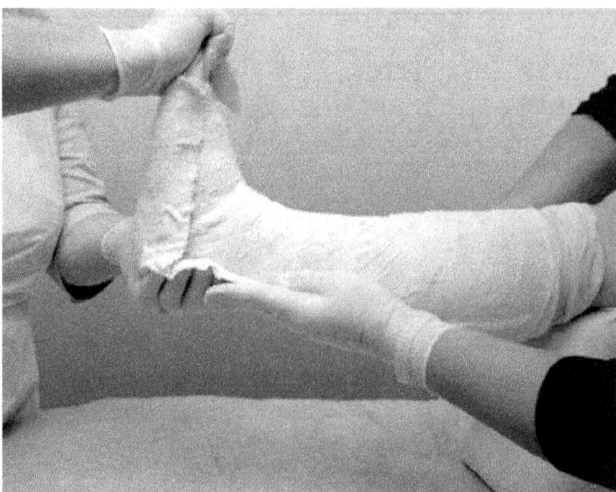

Fig. 15.

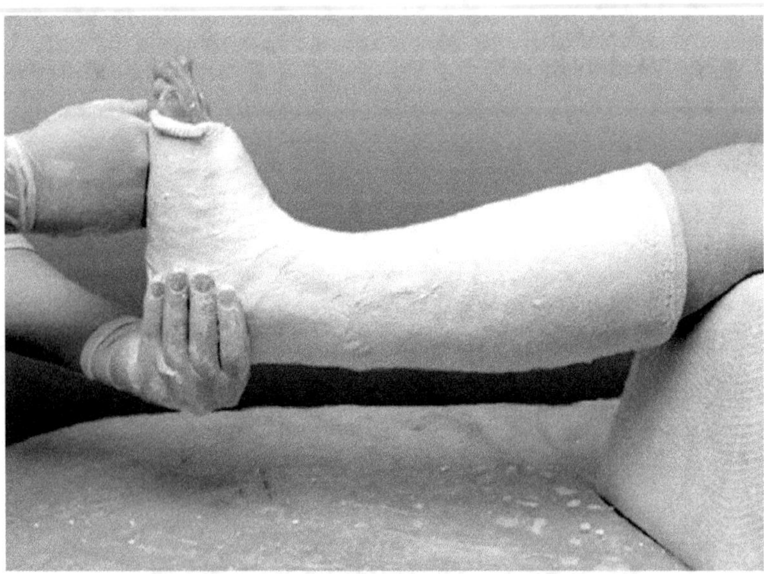

Fig. 16.

Below Knee Backslab (Adult)

Indications

- Acute fractures of tarsals / metatarsals
- Acute fractures of distal tibia/fibula
- Severe soft tissue injuries of foot, ankle or lower leg
- Refer to treatment profiles for relevant diagnostic tests.

Function

- Ankle immobilisation for acute lower leg, ankle or foot injuries.

Position

- Ankle at 90°
- Proximal limit – tibial tuberosity, and 1 cm below (distal to) fibular head to avoid damage to common peroneal nerve
- Distal limit – web of toes.

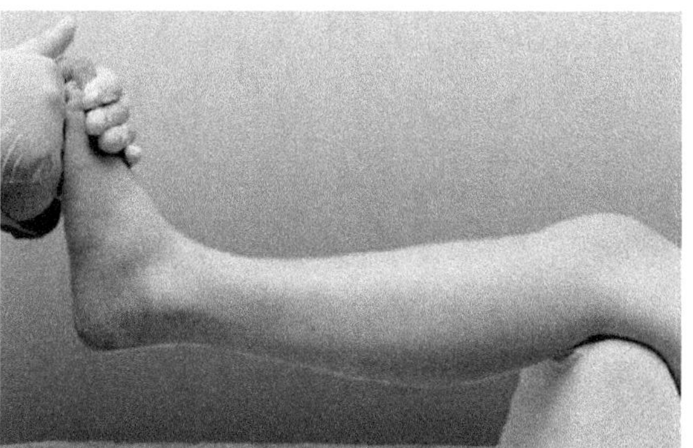

Fig. 17.

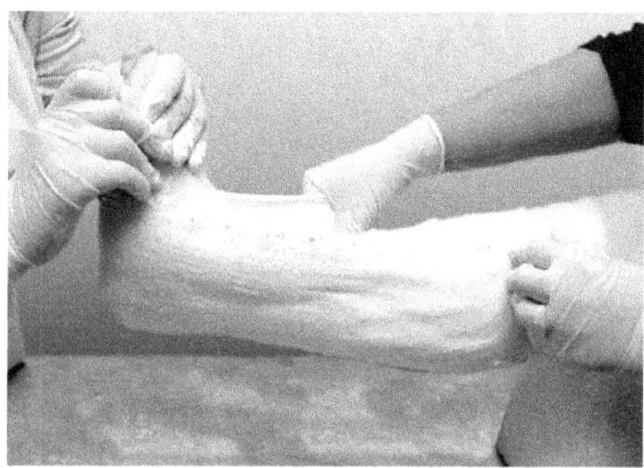

Fig. 18.

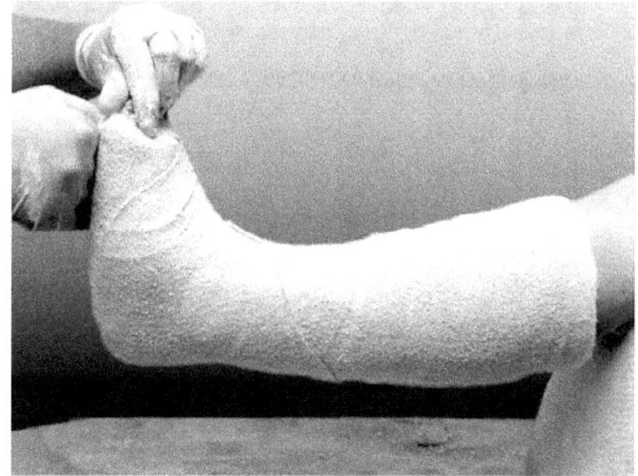

Fig. 19.

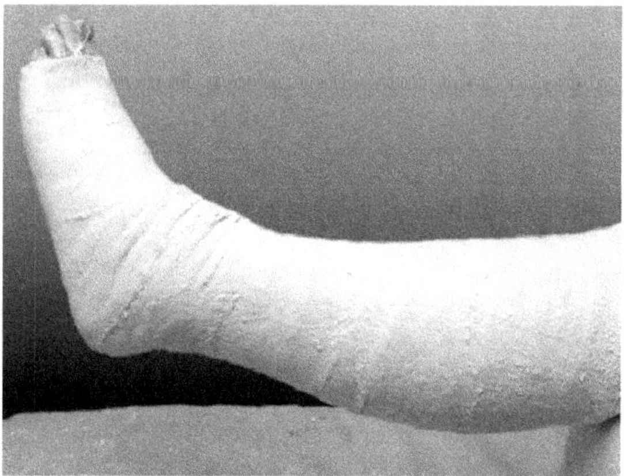

Fig. 20.

WRONG METHOD

Below knee cast incorrect

- POP proximal to tibial tuberosity
- Ankle inverted and plantarflexed
- POP too distal covering little toes
- POP wrinkled at ankle.

Volar Slab (Position of Function Splint)

Indications

- Finger and hand fractures
- Finger, hand, tendon and ligament injuries
- Severe soft tissue injuries of the hand

- Refer to treatment profiles for relevant diagnostic test.

Position

- Wrist 45° dorsiflexion
- MCP joints 90°
- Fingers fully extended
- Proximal limit - 4 cm distal to elbow crease
- Distal limit - to finger tips.

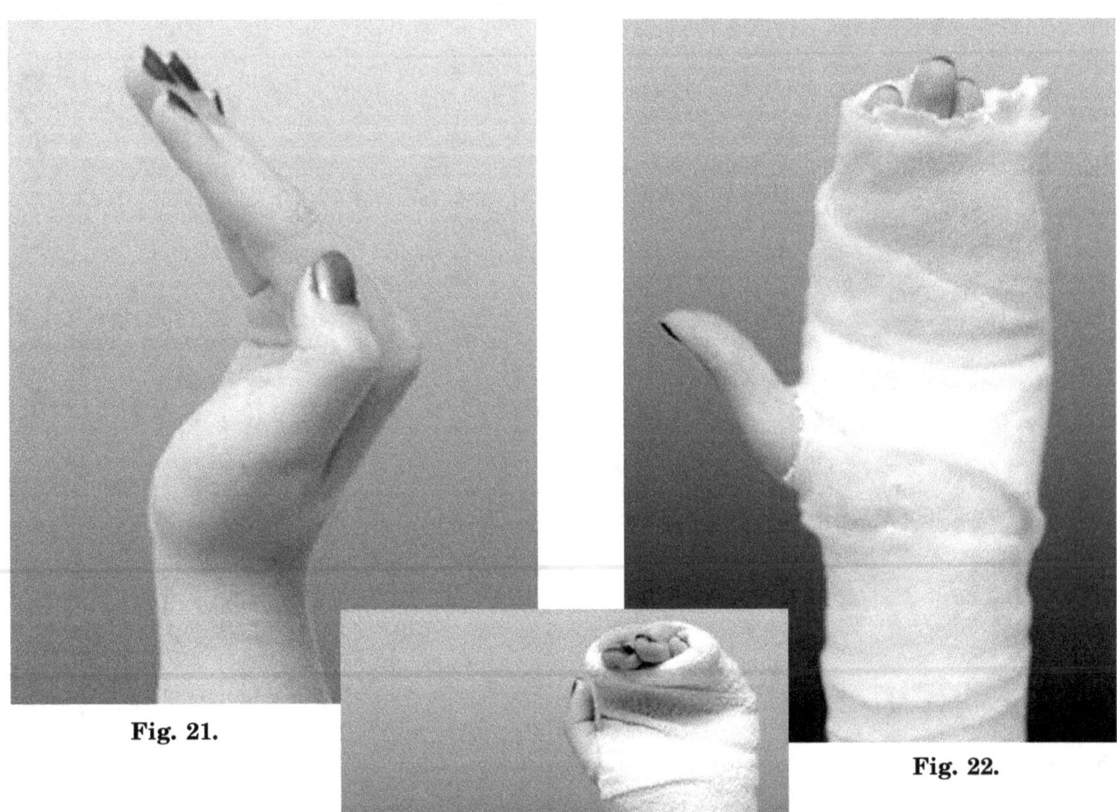

Fig. 21.

Fig. 22.

Fig. 23.

Scaphoid Cast

Indications

- Suspected or 'clinical' fracture of scaphoid
- Significant delay in X-ray or specialist assessment
- If fracture is confirmed or 'clinical', then referral to specialist should be arranged. In this case it may not be necessary to apply a full scaphoid cast as it will be removed for assessment
- Refer to treatment profiles for relevant diagnostic tests
- Many surgeons treat scaphoid fractures which do not require ORIF in BE complete cast, allowing some thumb function.

Position

- Thumb in opposition
- Middle finger and thumb forming an "O" (see Fig. below)

- Wrist in neutral
- Proximal limit – 4 cm distal to elbow crease
- Distal limit – to IP joint of thumb and proximal palmar crease and ability to

Application

- Ensure hand in correct position
- Cut POP slabs as shown
- Apply stockinet
- Apply layer of padding around thumb to IP joint and wrist and to 4 cm distal to elbow crease
- Apply reinforcing slabs to base of thumb
- Turn back padding
- Complete with POP bandage
- Cut bandage to ensure snug fit around thumb web
- Mould well while setting
- Ensure full movement of IP joint.

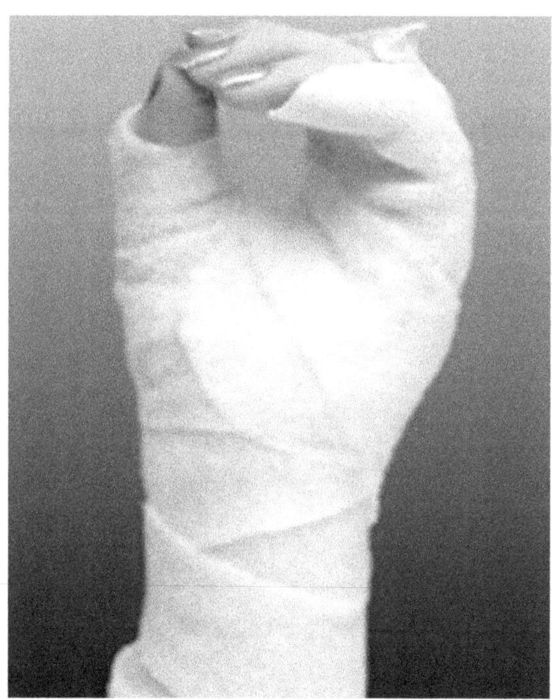

Fig. 24.

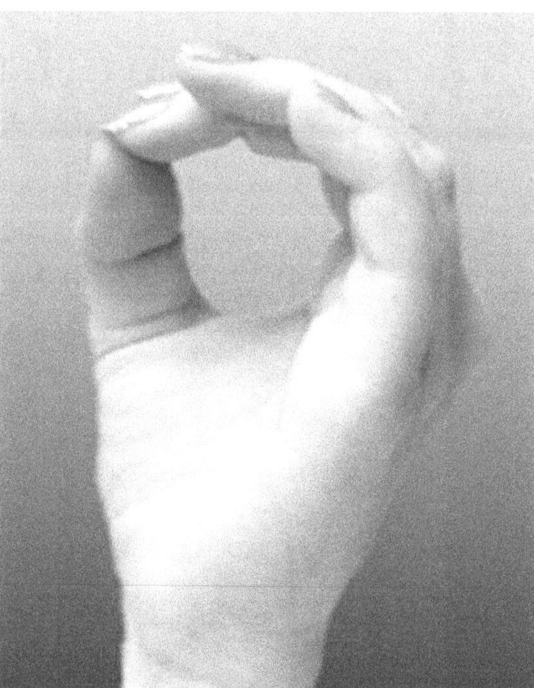

Fig. 25.

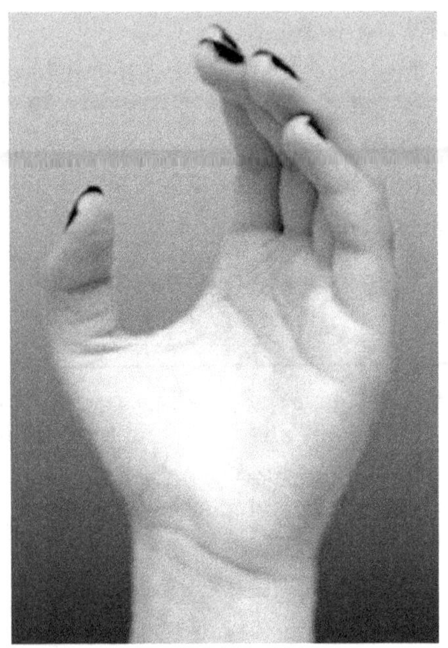

Fig. 26.

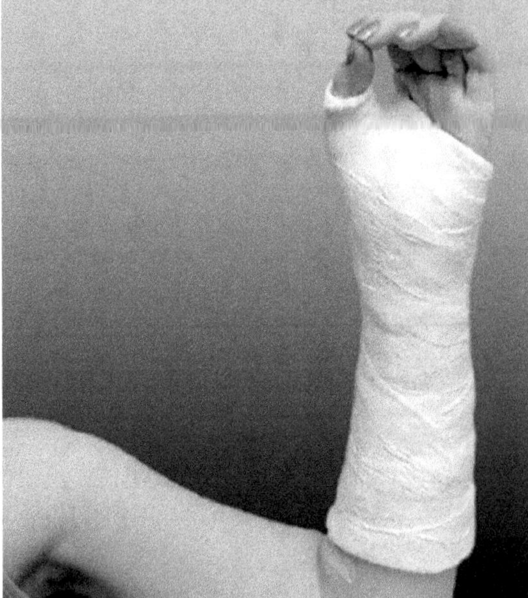

Fig. 27.

Bennett's Cast

Indications

- Fracture to base of thumb metacarpal (Bennett's fracture)
- See Treatment Profiles for relevant diagnostic tests.

Chapter-10

IMMEDIATE POSTOPERATIVE PATIENT CARE

Introduction

Surgical procedures are performed in many diverse settings, including surgeon's offices, ambulatory surgery centers, and hospital-based surgical suites and specialty units. In general, the selection of the surgical setting is influenced by:

- The anticipated complexity of the procedure
- The patient's health status
- Available technology, and
- Financial resources.

Regardless of the surgical setting or procedure, the patient should be observed and monitored postoperatively. The monitoring is performed in a controlled post surgical or post anaesthesia environment before the patient being transferred to a patient care unit or discharged from the facility. The postoperative phase of the surgical patient's perioperative experience begins after the surgical procedure is completed and the patient is admitted to a post-procedural area (usually the recovery room, RR).

Postoperative Observation of the Patient

The duration and type of postoperative observation and care will vary according to the following:

- Patient's condition (*e.g.*, alert and oriented *vs.* unresponsive)
- Need for physiologic support (*e.g.*, ventilator dependent, *vs.* awake and extubated)

- Complexity of the surgical procedure (*e.g.*, open laparotomy *vs.* laparoscopy)
- Type of anaesthesia administered (*e.g.*, a general inhalation agent *vs.* local infiltration)
- Prescribed period for monitoring parameters to evaluate physiologic status (*e.g.*, stable *vs.* unstable vital signs)

The Recovery Room Patient Care Personnel

Adequate personnel should be available to monitor patients and to provide appropriate care as needed. The education and training of a recovery room nurse should include knowledge of the following:

- Airway management techniques, including positioning, chin lift, jaw thrust, suctioning, bagging, and placement of an airway
- Circulatory assessment
- Neurological condition
- Anaesthetic agents and their action
- Medications and their action
- Most invasive and minimally invasive procedures. The nurses working in the recovery room should demonstrate competence in the following:
- Physical assessment (*e.g.*, heart and lung sounds)
- Recognition of physiologic complications (*e.g.*, airway obstruction, hypothermia, pain, nausea or vomiting, and/or oropharyngeal aspiration)

- Management of physiologic emergences (*e.g.*, airway obstruction, hemorrhage, cardiac arrest)
- Interpretation of monitoring data from electrocardiogram (ECG) and oximetry devices
- Application of cardiopulmonary resuscitation (CPR).

Admission of the Postoperative Patient to the Recovery Room

As the patient enters the recovery room (RR), his/her immediate physiologic and psychologic status is reported to the recovery room nurse by the accompanying personnel (usually the circulating nurse, assistant surgeon, or anaesthesia provider). The recovery room nurse observes the postoperative patient's wound (for bleeding), catheter, drain material, and intravenous infusions (whether they are in place). Then, the nurse monitors the vital signs of the patient as prescribed.

Patient Care Activities

The application of physiologic and psychosocial knowledge, principles of asepsis, and technical knowledge and skills are necessary to promote, restore, and maintain the patient's physiologic processes in a safe, comfortable and effective environment. Particular attention is given to monitoring oxygenation, ventilation and circulation. Recovery room care includes:

- Maintaining adequate ventilation
- Preventing shock, and
- Alleviating pain

Patients are evaluated continually by appropriate monitoring methods and frequent observations by nurses. Clinical evaluation of each patient's status through listening, watching, and feeling is augmented by electronic monitoring devices if available. As in all other patient care areas, standard precautions are carried out for the disposal of needles and the handling of any item contaminated by blood and body fluids. Hand washing is essential after each patient contact

to prevent cross contamination. Family members are notified when a patient is admitted to the recovery room (RR). This lets them know the surgical procedure is complete, which helps to relieve the anxiety experienced during the hours of waiting.

Documentation

Institutional policies and procedures should be followed in documenting the care given in the recovery room. Observations of respiratory and circulatory functions and level of consciousness are recorded at frequent intervals. Postoperative physiologic and psychologic status are documented at the time of any significant event (*e.g.*, the administration of medication), as well as routinely at 5- to 7-minutes interval for the first hour and at 15- to 30-minutes intervals for the second hour and thereafter.

Discharge of the Post-operative Patient from the Recovery Room

Most patients remain in the recovery room (RR) for at least one hour or until they have sufficiently recovered from anaesthesia and that their vital signs have stabilized and they are capable of reasonable self-care. The patient's condition is scored according to *vital signs, activity level*, and *consciousness*.

After discharge from the recovery room, the patient is transported to a patient care unit (ward) or an intensive care unit (if present) or to home with follow-up appointment. A physician is responsible for the patient's discharge from the recovery room.

The recovery room will be divided into an appropriate number of bays (areas), each of which equipped to receive a patient on his/her trolley or bed. The bays should be separated by curtains which can be drawn to provide privacy for nursing and medical procedures and withdrawn to allow easy observation of the patient. Each bay should be spacious enough to give easy access of staff to the patient and also room for bulky equipment such as a resuscitation trolley or mobile X-ray machine. There should be an oxygen outlet and at least one, preferably two, vacuum points in each bay. Two vacuum sources are preferable since a patient may require suction to be applied continuously to a surgical drain while suction may also be required at the same time to remove secretions from the airway.

The other very important facility which each bay requires is an adequate number of electrical outlets. At least six in each bay should be available, since certain patients will require a number of items of electrical apparatus to be in use simultaneously. For example, a patient may require a pulmonary ventilator, an electrocardiograph monitor, a blood warmer, a drip controller, etc. Thus, it is easy to see why a large number of electrical outlets are required.

Equipment for monitoring
- Electrocardiograph
- Blood pressure apparatus
- Central venous pressure
- Temperature
- Urinary output.

Equipment for intravenous infusion
- Supply of intravenous (IV) fluids
- Plasma substitutes
- Refrigerator for storing blood for transfusion
- Intravenous giving sets
- Intravenous cannulae
- Central venous catheters
- Drip controllers or infusion pumps
- Blood warmers
- Pressure infusers (for pressurizing bags of intravenous fluid for rapid transfusion)
- Blood filters.

General
- Syringes and needles
- Swabs
- Preparations for cleaning skin prior to injections, etc.
- Forms and appropriate sample tubes for biochemistry, hematology, blood transfusion, bacteriology.
- Requirements.

Drugs for resuscitation trolley
There will be a small range of drugs required in acute cardiac or respiratory emergences:
- Sodium bicarbonate solution 8.4%
- Adrenaline 1:1000
- Calcium chloride 10%
- Isoprenaline
- Atropine
- Lignocaine for intravenous use
- Beta-blocking drugs *e.g.*, propranolol
- A cardiac glycoside, *e.g.*, digoxin
- An antihistamine, *e.g.*, promethazine
- A bronchodilator, *e.g.*, aminophylline
- Antinarcotics agents, *e.g.*, naloxone
- Hydrocortisone
- Sterile water for injection when necessary.

Drugs in the Recovery Room
In addition to the list of drugs required for acute resuscitation (a full supply of which should be available in addition to emergency supply), a wide range of drugs are required in the recovery area and will include many of those drugs normally used in the surgical wards. Thus, a comprehensive list is impractical here. The most frequently used will be:
- Analgesic drugs such as morphine, pethidine, etc.
- Antibiotics
- Local anesthetic agents
- Insulin for diabetic patients
- Heparin, corticosteroids
- Diuretics and anti-emetics.

Chapter-11

PRE-OPERATIVE CARE STEPS

Identify Features and Functions of the Surgical Theatre

Identified traffic patterns in the surgical suite:

(a) unrestricted area

(b) semi-restricted area

(c) restricted area

Identified placement, function, and operation of each of the following:

(a) surgical theatre bed

(b) mayo stands

(c) instrument table

(d) overhead table

(e) ring stand

(f) small tables

(g) supply cabinet

(h) kick bucket

(i) surgical theatre lights

(j) suction machine

(k) electrosurgical unit

(l) x-ray view box

Perform a Surgical Hand Scrub

1. Prepared for the surgical hand scrub.
2. Performed a preliminary wash and cleansed each nail under running water.
3. Timed the surgical hand scrub for fingers, hands, and forearms for the recommended number of minutes.
4. Treated each finger, hand, and arm as a four-sided object.
5. Rinsed the hands and arms keeping hands above elbows at all times.
6. Entered the surgical theatre by backing through the door.
7. Dried hands and arms using aseptic techniques.

Position the Surgical Patient

1. Patient identified per RN.
2. Confirmed the operative site and the proposed position.
3. Assembled the necessary equipment for positioning.
4. Observed safety measures in positioning the patient.
5. Placed the patient in the following positions:
   (a) dorsal recumbent (supine)
   (b) lithotomy
   (c) prone
6. Accommodated anomalies and physical defects, if applicable.
7. Avoided unnecessary exposure of the body.
8. Observed patient position once again to determine if it adhered to physiological principles before skin preparation and draping.

Perform Gowning and Gloving

1. Donned gown:

(a) grasped gown and lifted up-did not drag.

(b) stepped away from stand.

(c) allowed gown to unfold with inside facing wearer.

(d) extended arms in front at shoulder level and placed hands in armholes.

(e) slid arms into sleeves:

    1. did not shake or flip sleeves

    2. grasped at sleeve/stockinette seam

    3. kept fingers inside stockinette

(f) kept hands above elbows

Circulator assisted:

1. reached inside shoulder and arm seams so hands are covered by gown

2. pulled sleeves on, leaving cuffs over hands

3. tied inner tie

4. fastened neck fasteners

2. Donned gloves:

(a) opened glove packet using mitten—hands (gown covering hands)

(b) picked up glove by folded edge—did not drag off wrapper

(c) stepped back from table

(d) did not allow glove to touch unsterile area

(e) kept hands above waist

(f) kept hands inside stockinette cuff

(g) placed glove palm down on the inner aspect of the left wrist fingers towards elbow

(h) grasped folded edge of glove cuff though the stockinette gown cuff with the left hand

(i) grasped the top edge of the glove cuff with the right hand and pulled it forward and over the left hand, placing the cuff on the outer aspect of the left wrist

(j) pulled gown sleeve and glove on at same time

(k) did not pull gown cuff out of glove

(l) repeated above steps for second glove

Identify Names and Uses of Surgical Instruments

1. Correctly chose instruments according to a list provided by the instructor.

2. Identified the type of instrument.

3. Identified box lock joint.

4. Identified ratchet.

5. Identified jaw.

Prepare and Engage Accessory Surgical Equipment — the Electrosurgical Unit (Cautery Machine)

1. Ensured that the patient was not in contact with metal parts of the OR bed.

2. Connected the unit to the electrical source.

3. Grounded the patient by placing the cautery pad:

    (a) under the buttocks or diagonally across thigh

    (b) on a (relatively) hair-free area of skin

    (c) after inspecting the skin for scars, rashes, or breaks

    (d) avoiding area over scar tissue

4. Preset the controls according to surgeon's instructions.

5. Positioned the unit for convenience.

6. Attached the cautery pad cord to the unit.

7. Attached cautery tip cord (active electrode) to the unit.

8. Positioned the footplate, if required.

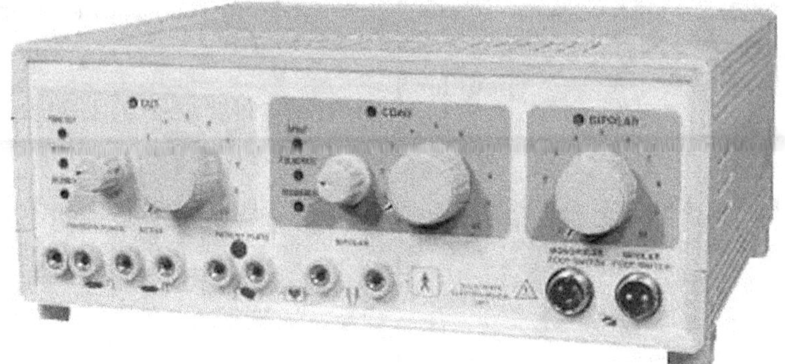

Fig. 1: *Cautery Machine*

Perform Preoperative Skin Care

A. Abdominal

1. Prepared supplies and poured solutions.
2. Prepared the patient.
   (*a*) received permission from the anaesthetist
   (*b*) turned on the light
   (*c*) exposed the area
   (*d*) placed the patient in the appropriate position:
   - arms secured
   - legs uncrossed
   - leg straps in place
   (*e*) inspected the area to be prepped
3. Checked the supplies.
4. Moved the prep stand and kick bucket into position.
5. Draped the area with towels:
   (*a*) opposite side first
   (*b*) top and bottom area boundaries
   (*c*) side nearest you last
6. Donned sterile gloves.
7. Cleansed umbilicus with sponges or applicators moistened with prep solution.
8. Began skin prep:
   (*a*) started at incisional site and worked outward
   (*b*) discarded the sponge and repeated the procedure
   (*c*) did not retrace
9. Opened towel and placed on prepped skin and blotted the area dry. Patted gently over the entire area.

B. Perineal

1. Prepared the supplies and poured the solutions.
2. Prepared the patient:
   (*a*) received permission from the anaesthetist
   (*b*) turned on the light
   (*c*) exposed the area
   (*d*) placed the patient in the appropriate position:
   - arms secured
   - legs in stirrups (needs another person to help)
   - safety straps in place
   (*e*) inspected area to be prepped

Prepare and engage accessory surgical equipment – the pneumatic tourniquet

3. Checked supplies.
4. Moved the prep stand and kick bucket into position.
5. Placed fully opened towel under the buttocks.
6. Donned sterile gloves.
7. Began skin prep:
   (*a*) started at the hypogastric region and worked down to the mon pubis with lathered sponges

(*b*) discarded sponges

(*c*) did not retrace

(*d*) continued prep on inner thighs, vulva and perineum finishing with the anus

(*e*) discarded sponges when appropriate

8. Blotted area dry with an open towel.

9. Removed towel without dragging it over the prepped area.

10. Applied antiseptic solution using the established sequence.

11. Removed towel from under buttocks.

12. Disassembled prep set; discarded linens, collected trash.

Prepare and Engage Accessory Surgical Equipment – the Pneumatic Tourniquet

1. Protected the patient's skin by placing protective padding around the extremity under the tourniquet.

2. Protected vulnerable neuro-vascular structures in applying the tourniquet cuff.

3. Recorded location.

4. Set and recorded pressure setting.

5. Elevated extremity to promote venous return.

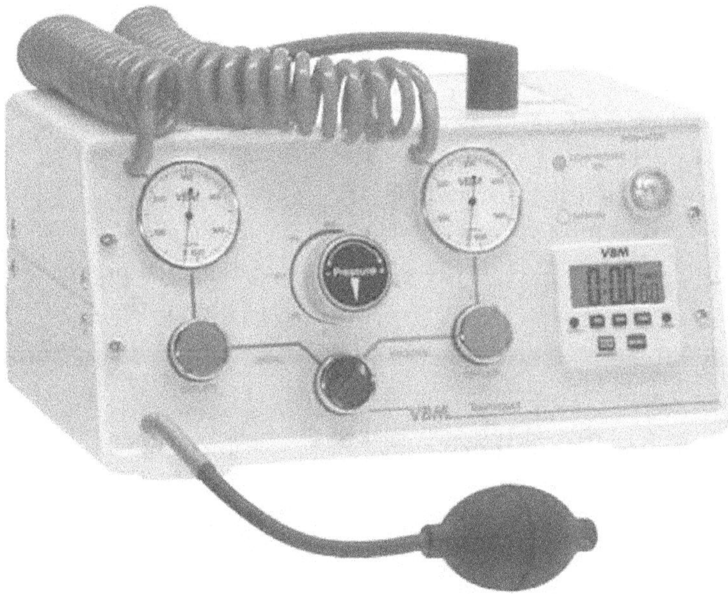

Fig. 2: *Tourniquet*

6. Checked with the anaesthetist prior to inflating or deflating the tourniquet.

7. Recorded time:

(*a*) of inflation

(*b*) of deflation

8. Notified surgeon when tourniquet had been on for one hour and every 15 minutes thereafter.

Prepare and Engage Accessory Surgical Equipment – Endoscopic Equipment

1. Connected the machine to electrical source.

2. Ensured that power sources, gas supply and lights worked.

3. Set gas flow and pressure gauges appropriately and checked presence of filter (if required).

4. Connected insufflation tubing and ensured proper functioning.

5. Connected and checked fiberoptic cable for adequate light transmission.

6. Completed white balancing procedure.

Prepare and Engage Accessory Surgical Equipment – Air-Powered Equipment

1. Ensured that attachments and blades were seated and locked in handle before activating power.

2. Set safety latch in position.

As circulator

3. Received power cord and attached it to the wall outlet or nitrogen tank.

4. Opened air source.

5. Set pressure while the air-powered instrument was running or in used.

Arrange Sterile Instruments and Supplies

1. Arranged furniture.

2. Obtained necessary sterile supplies.

3. Checked supplies for integrity of packaging, date and change in processing indicator.

4. Opened supplies properly and in appropriate order.

5. Scrubbed, gowned, and gloved.

6. Set up gown table.

7. Checked linen pack for sterility.

8. Draped Mayo stand. (Not for perineal procedure).

9. Put Mayo tray in place. (Not for perineal procedure).

10. Arranged the instrument table:

   (a) picked up all basins and placed on the instrument table

   (b) arranged the drapes in order of use

   (c) placed sponges correctly

   (d) smoothed out creases in table drape

   (e) rolled a towel and placed on table to assist in placement of instruments

11. Set up instruments and accessory items on the instrument table:

   (a) removed retractors from pan and placed on table

   (b) lifted the string of instruments from the pan and placed the handles over the rolled towel

   (c) sorted out sutures and needles

   (d) placed accessory equipment appropriately

12. Counted with the circulator.

Drape a Patient

1. Protected sterile attire during draping procedure.

2. Draped for a laparotomy following the correct sequence:

   (a) selected proper supplies

   (b) placed the 1st drape closest to self

   (c) placed the 2nd drape below the incision site

   (d) placed the 3rd drape above the incision site

   (e) placed the 4th drape on the side opposite self

   (f) placed the barrier drape below the incision site

   (g) placed the laparotomy sheet so as to provide adequate exposure of the incisional site and a smooth covering for the operative field

   (h) secured tubings with non-perforating clamps

   (i) did not readjust drape once it had been placed

   (j) reinforced drapes as necessary to maintain sterility of field.

3. Draped for a perineal procedure following the correct sequence:

  (*a*) selected the proper supplies

  (*b*) opened, made a cuff for hands, and placed the medium drape with enclosed barrier drape under the buttocks

  (*c*) placed the folded small drape over the pubic area

  (*d*) prepared the lithotomy drape for application

  (*e*) opened the drape to allow bottom to drop towards the floor

  (*f*) opened the folds of the drape sufficiently to allow it to be eased over first one leg and then the other, then the remainder of the drape is placed over the abdomen (assistance of the circulator is required)

  (*g*) secured tubings with non-perforating clamps

  (*h*) did not readjust drape once it had been placed

  (*i*) reinforced drapes as necessary to maintain sterility of field

4. Prepared instruments for immediate use:

(Abdominal procedures)

  (*a*) placed instruments on Mayo tray in order of use

  (*b*) folded 3 × 3 sponges and placed on sponge sticks

  (*c*) placed abdominal sponge in bowl

  (*d*) folded and placed 2 abdominal sponges on Mayo tray

  (*e*) prepared a ligature reel and placed on Mayo tray

  (*f*) prepared the first suture

  (*g*) placed suction, cautery, pocket drape, nonpiercing towel clips, and light handles on the Mayo tray

5. Prepared instruments for immediate use:

(Perineal procedures)

  (*a*) placed instruments at the front of the table in order of use

  (*b*) prepared 8 × 4 sponges

  (*c*) prepare Auvard speculum

  (*d*) prepared first suture

Manage Surgical Specimens

Routine specimens:

(a) Scrub:

1. received each specimen in a basin or medicine glass; did not place the specimen on a sponge

2. did not clamp the specimen

3. kept each specimen separate

4. handed the specimens to the circulator one at a time

5. handed each specimen to the circulator in the basin, on a wrapper, or on a towel

6. told the circulator the name of each specimen

7. wiped his/her hands

(b) Circulator:

1. donned disposable gloves

2. placed each specimen in an

3. appropriate container

4. accurately labelled each container immediately

5. covered the specimens with formalin

6. accurately completed the laboratory forms

7. took the specimens and forms to the designated area

8. washed his/her hands

Demonstrate the Safe Handling of Sterile Sutures, Sharps and Surgical Instruments

1. Passed threaded suture:

  (*a*) placed needle on needle holder

  (*b*) threaded needle

(c) grasped needle holder near top of shank

(d) passed needle holder with handle in surgeon's palm with needle pointing up toward surgeon's thumb

(e) let suture material hang free over back of hand

(f) kept suture ends out of surgeon's palm

(g) held tail of suture with free hand

2. Passed free tie:

(a) grasped suture at each end

(b) stretched suture taut

(c) came in and under surgeon's extended fingers

(d) passed to surgeon's hand with upward motion

3. Passed straight needle:

(a) grasped needle close to point

(b) passed needle to surgeon, eyed end first

(c) controlled the suture ends

4. Applied scalpel blade to handle:

(a) faced away from other persons

(b) aimed blade away from self

(c) grasped handle in left hand

(d) grasped needle holder in right hand.

INSTRUMENT CARE INSTRUCTIONS

Instrument Longevity Through Proper Care

Maintaining the Surface

New Instruments

Newly purchased instruments must be cleaned, lubricated and autoclaved immediately before use.

Correct Use

Obvious as it sounds, it bears repeating: instruments are designed for a particular purpose and should be used only for that purpose. Even the strongest instrument can be damaged when used in appropriately, *i.e.*, when a nail splitter is used to cut wire.

Water and Stainless Steel

Ordinary tap water contains minerals that can cause discoloration and staining. Therefore, we recommend the use of distilled water for cleaning, disinfecting, sterilizing and rinsing instruments. To avoid staining, use a cleaning solution with a pH near neutral (7). Instruments should be placed in distilled water immediately after use. They should never be placed in saline solution, as it may cause corrosion and eventually irreversible pitting.

Manual Cleaning and Soaking

When handling instruments, be very careful not to damage their fine tips and mechanisms. If instruments have been exposed to blood, tissue, saline or other foreign matter, they must be rinsed in warm (not hot) water before these substances are allowed to dry. Failure to do so may result in rust. After rinsing, immerse them in a cleaning and disinfecting solution. Because many compounds, including certain chemicals, are highly corrosive to stainless steel, rinse and dry instruments immediately, in case they have come in contact with any potentially harmful substances.

If no ultrasonic cleaner is available, clean the instrument very carefully. Pay particular attention when cleaning box locks, serrations, hinges and other hard to-each areas. What's more, use nylon (not steel) brushes, such as KM 39-684, and warm (not hot) cleaning solutions. Follow the manufacturer's instructions for the preparation of the cleaning solutions. Remember to change these solutions daily.

Ultrasonic Cleaning

Ultrasonic cleaning is the most effective and efficient way to clean instruments. To maximize its effectiveness, instruments should be cleaned of all visible debris before they are put into an ultrasonic cleaner. Please note that chrome-plated instruments may rust if they are not dried and lubricated immediately after sterilization. In addition we recommend the following:

- Do not mix dissimilar metals, *e.g.*, chrome and stainless, in the same cycle.
- Use only designated cleaners.
- Open all instruments so ratchets and box locks are accessible.
- When possible, disassemble instruments for optimal cleaning.
- Avoid piling instruments on top of each other when loading and follow the manufacturer's instructions.
- Remove and rinse off instruments immediately after the cycle is finished.
- Allow instruments to air-dry thoroughly.
- Lubricate all moving parts after cleaning and before sterilization.
- Use only surgical lubricants, which can penetrate the instruments during the sterilization process.
- Change the water in the cleaner regularly.

Instrument Checkup

The best time to review the condition of instruments is after they have been cleaned and lubricated and have cooled off. Consider the following:

Function

"Sharps" must cut cleanly (resharpen if needed) and close properly. Check for burrs along the cutting edges. Needle holders and clamps must engage properly and meet correctly at the tips.

Surface

Carefully inspect surfaces for any sign of staining, cracking or other irregularities.

Common sources of staining are:

- Inadequate cleaning
- Mixing dissimilar metals
- Impurities in the water
- Unsuitable or improper preparation and usage of cleaning and disinfecting or maintenance agents
- Noncompliance with operating procedures of cleaning and sterilizing equipment

Lubrication and Autoclaving

All instruments must be properly cleaned before autoclaving. Then their moving parts, such as box locks and hinges, should be well lubricated. Be careful to use surgical lubricants and not industrial oils. Always sterilize instruments in the open, unlocked position. We recommend that instruments be wrapped in cloth and then placed in the container, or that a cloth be put on the bottom of the pan to absorb moisture. The cloth should be pH(7) neutral and have no residue of detergents. Finally, avoid sudden cooling. Instruments should be allowed to airdry, not rinsed or dried off.

Cold Sterilizing or Disinfecting

Prolonged immersion in disinfecting or sterilizing solution can damage surgical instruments. Do not soak instruments for longer than 20 minutes. To render the instruments sterile and ready for use, use an autoclave cycle.

Caution

Instruments with tungsten carbide inserts, such as wire cutters, needle holders and TC scissors, should never be immersed in sterilizing solutions containing benzyl ammonium chloride (BAC). BAC will soften and dissolve the tungsten carbide. Never use bleach as it will cause severe pitting.

Storage

Once instruments are thoroughly dry, store them in a clean, dry environment. Never put them in areas where chemicals may emit corrosive vapours or where temperature and moisture variations could cause condensation on the instruments.

Medic Quick Instrument Care Checklist

1. Rinse and soak soiled instruments immediately after use. Thoroughly clean before autoclaving.
2. Clean, autoclave and sterilize instruments in an open position.
3. Do not stack or entangle instruments.
4. Follow the manufacturer's recommendations when using equipment and cleaning solutions.
5. Keep instruments properly lubricated.
6. Inspect instruments regularly.

Tips for Troubleshooting

This guide is intended as a quick reference to handle many of the most basic questions and problems regarding surgical instruments.

Staining

Staining is most frequently the result of improper or inadequate cleaning.

Stains can be caused by mineral deposits in the water or electrolysis.

Instruments should be cleaned in distilled water to avoid this. Staining should not be confused with rusting.

Blue Stains

This discolouration is usually caused by cold disinfecting or sterilizing solutions. Solutions should be changed frequently, as corrosion may otherwise occur. Distilled water will also inhibit discolouration.

Black Stains

This discolouration can occur when instruments are exposed to ammonia, which is present in many hospital cleaners, and are not then adequately rinsed. When possible, avoid using cleaning agents with ammonia, and always rinse instruments thoroughly.

Black stains can sometimes be caused by residues of chemicals used to clean the steam pipes.

Brown Stains

Brown stains are probably the result of oxidation and should not be confused with rust (see Rust/Corrosion 13.4). It forms naturally on stainless steel and helps prevent atmospheric corrosion. It should not be a cause of concern.

Spotting

Spotting is usually the result of improper cleaning. It may be caused by the water in which instruments are washed or by detergent residues in the wrapping material.

Light Spots

Mineral-rich tap water or detergent residues may leave deposits. Rinsing the instrument in distilled water will generally remove these deposits; if this fails, they can usually be cleaned off using a special, nonabrasive stainless steel cleaner or stain remover.

To avoid this problem, thoroughly dry instruments in the autoclave and avoid using cloths with detergent residues.

Dark Spots

Like light spots, these are usually caused by mineral deposits in the water used to clean, rinse and sterilize instruments. To avoid this problem, always use distilled water.

Rustlike Film

This film may be caused by residue in steam pipes. Unfortunately, little can be done in this situation.

The film may also be caused by chemical compounds used to treat water. As a result, iron may be deposited on instruments. Take this up with hospital engineering staff. Use distilled water to clean instruments.

Miscellaneous Stains and Spots

Spots and stains may also be caused if too much or the wrong kind of detergent is used to wash the instruments. Use a cleaner formulated specifically for surgical instruments.

Rust/Corrosion

If treated properly, stainless steel does not usually rust. Brown discolouration, which looks like rust to the ordinary eye, is often mistaken for rust.

Is it Rust?

A quick test to check whether you are dealing with rust or discolouration is to take an ordinary rubber eraser and try to rub away the imperfection—if you are able to do so, the problem is not with the instrument, and you should look into possible causes in the care and handling of the instrument.

If the instrument is corroding, it can be seen with a magnifying glass, because small pits begin to form in the steel. Such instruments should be removed from circulation and no longer used.

Corrosive Substances

Rusting may be the result of exposure to salts, saline, blood, iodine, chloride, bleach or other aggressive substances or due to the use of abrasives in the cleaning process, which can wear away the passive layers. Surgical instruments should only be cleaned with solutions which the manufacturer has specifically stated are safe for such use.

Inadequate Cleaning

Corrosion can also be the result of inadequate cleaning. If blood or other bodily secretions are allowed to remain on the instruments, corrosion may occur. This is particularly a problem in hard-to-clean areas such as jaw serrations, box locks and ratchets. Instruments should be cleaned in the open position, and whenever possible should be disassembled.

Instruments should also be cleaned in distilled water. Deposits may form on instruments if they are washed in tap water, which may cause spotting and eventually corrosion.

Incomplete Drying

Incomplete drying may also end in corrosion—instruments should not be removed from the autoclave until they have been thoroughly dried.

Lubrication

Instruments should always be carefully lubricated. Failure to do so may result in wear, which could lead to corrosion.

Improper Usage

Improper usage is another common cause of corrosion. When corrosion appears at stress points in an instrument, *e.g.*, at the jaws or box lock, this may be a sign of improper usage.

Improper Marking

Rust can also be caused by improper marking of the instrument with an engraver. Never mark anything on a box lock since it may weaken it.

Rust Transfer

Rust transfer can occur when instruments made of dissimilar metals come into contact for an extended period of time—to avoid this, wash and sterilize instruments of different metals separately.

Transfer rust can usually be removed with a rubber eraser. If neglected, however, rust may begin to mar the surface.

Pitting

Pitting may be caused by the use of improper cleaning agents, such as saline or bleach. Use only cleaners formulated for use with surgical instruments. It may also be the result of the use of improper concentrations of cleaning agents, or cleaning agents which have a pH level which is too acidic or alkaline.

Avoid using these kinds of detergents. The optimal pH for a cleaning fluid is close to neutral, ca. pH(7).

Pitting may also occur in the ultrasonic cleaner if instruments of different metals are cleaned in the same cycle. This can also occur in the autoclaving process.

Broken Instrument

An instrument should not normally break if it is being used for its intended purpose. Breakage is likely the result of either an instrument being used for something other than what it was designed for, or being used to perform a task beyond its capacity, *e.g.*, a wire cutter with a maximum cutting capacity of .045" is used to cut a wire of a larger size.

Another cause of breakage comes during the ultrasonic or autoclaving process. Instruments should be cleaned and autoclaved in the open, not locked, position.

In the locked position, the heat may make the instrument expand and crack the box lock.

Chapter-12

GLOSSARY

Abduction: To draw away from the center line of the body.

Abrasive: Substance which removes or deteriorates a surface by friction.

Absorbable suture: Any suture that is absorbed by body tissue.

Acetabulum: The large, cup-shaped cavity at which the femur, or thigh bone, joins the hip.

Adduction: To draw toward the center line of the body.

Analgesia: The absence of pain.

Anastomosis: An opening between two normally distinct spaces or organs; used in surgery to refer to the joining of two hollow structures with suture.

Anaesthetic: An agent that produces analgesia.

Angled: Bent, not straight.

Anodized: Aluminum which has been specially treated through an electrochemical process which forms a protective oxide layer, rendering it corrosion resistant; used to make instrument racks; the oxide layer of anodized aluminum may be coloured.

Antibiotic: A drug formed from chemical substances produced by a micro-organism that kills or inhibits the growth of other micro-organisms.

Antiseptic: An agent that is used to reduce the amount or arrest the growth of pathogenic micro-organisms on animate (living) surfaces.

AO: *Arbeitsgemeinschaft fuer Osteosynthesefragen*; an international organization dedicated to research of internal bone fixation (osteosynthesis), as well as instrument design for and documentation of osteosynthesis.

Approximate: Tips instrument tips have proper alignment.

Arthrodesis: Fusion of a joint in a surgical procedure.

Arthroplasty: Surgical reconstruction of a joint.

Arthroscopy: Examination of the inside of a joint with an arthroscope.

Articular: Pertaining to a joint.

Articulate: Divided into or separated by joints.

Asepsis: Absence of micro-organisms that cause disease; freedom from infection; exclusion of micro-organisms.

Aseptic: Free of disease, causing micro-organisms.

Aspirate: To remove fluid or gas from a cavity or joint area using suction.

Atraumatic: Not having a crushing or biting effect on tissue.

Attire: Cloths to be worn in the operating room.

Autoclave: Machine for the sterilization of surgical instruments.

Bayonet: A blade that is offset (bent) from the axis of the handle.

Biopsy: The removal and examination of tissue from a living body.

Blank: First stage in the actual manufacture of an instrument; involves the creation of the basic form of the instrument; may be created through hot or cold forging.

Bone graft: Use of bone tissue to reconstruct an area of missing bone box lock the area of an instrument at which the male and female parts of the instrument are joined.

Bunionectomy: The resection of a bunion, an abnormal prominence at the midsection of the first metatarsal head (below the big toe) calcaneus bone of the heel.

Caliper: A compass with bent or curved jaws used to take measurements cancellous spongy and latticelike (soft) bone.

Cancellous: Bone ends of long bones, most of flat and short bones (latticelike bone)

Cannula: A tube for insertion into a duct or cavity; used to drain fluids.

Carpal: Pertaining to the group of eight small, short bones which form the wrist.

Cartilage: White substance covering joint surfaces which can be compressed, allowing for motion without friction.

Catheter: Instrument used to remove fluids from a cavity in the body cavitation a process to clean instruments using sound waves in an ultrasonic cleaner.

Cerclage wire: Used in the treatment of long, spiral fractures; it is placed around the bone and tightened; used also in other cases in which temporary fixation is required.

Cervical: Refers to the area at the upper portion of the spine chisel wedgelike instrument with a blade, generally used with a mallet to cut and shape bone.

Chondral pertaining to cartilage

Chromic salts: Chemicals used in the treatment of catgut that cause it to resist absorption.

Cleaning agents: Detergents designed for the removal of protein soils, a necessary step in cleaning instruments.

Closed reduction: To set a broken bone by compression.

Complex fracture: Situation in which, after reduction, there is still no contact between the main fragments.

Compound fracture: An open fracture in which the bone is broken completely across corrosion the gradual wearing away of a surface; may be caused chemically.

Contaminated: Soiled or infected by micro-organisms.

Corrosive: Causing the gradual dissolving and deterioration of a substance, especially by chemicals.

Cortex external: Layer of cancellous bone or middle layer of long bones cortical pertaining to the outer layer of cancellous bone (cortex) or middle layer of long bones (hard bones).

Cortical bone: Solid portion of a bone; surrounds medullary canal cranium the skull or brain pan.

Critical dimension: Area of a surgical instrument which must correspond very closely to product specifications, as in the parts that need to mate with other parts, e.g., QC handle, screwdrivers, etc. curette spoon-shaped instrument used to scrape, shape and remove bone.

Cross-contamination: A process whereby infection or disease is spread from one source to another.

Curette: A spoon-shaped instrument used to scrape tissue from a surface.

Curved continuously: Deviating from a straight line, as in a curved blade or handle.

Debridement: Removal of foreign material or contaminated tissue to expose surrounding healthy tissue.

Decontamination: Process that makes inanimate objects safer to be handled by staff before cleaning.

Defamation: A derogatory statement made by someone about another.

Dilator: Instrument used to stretch or enlarge an opening dissect to cut or separate tissue.

Disinfectant: An agent that kills or inactivates micro-organisms on inanimate surfaces.

Dissector: Instrument used to cut apart or separate tissue distilled water purified liquid condensed from boiled water; preferred choice for instrument cleaning.

Double-action: Applies power in two directions, used in instrument mechanism to increase surgeon's power and to control and reduce fatigue dull blunted, not sharp.

Electrolysis: Decomposition of a chemical compound into its ions by the passage of an electrical current through a solution of it (electrolyte).

Electrolytic: Having to do with electrolysis or with an electrolyte elevator instrument used for lifting or retaining at a greater height; sharp versions are used to strip the periosteum.

Etching: Process by which instruments are marked to facilitate.

Ethylene oxide: A gas used in the sterilization of items.

Excision: The cutting away or removal of tissue, bone, etc.

Fascia: Sheet of fibrous tissue encasing the body beneath the skin, enclosing muscles and muscle groups, and separating their layers.

Fasciotomy: Removal of the fascia.

Femur: Bone of the thigh.

Fenestrated: Pierced with one or more openings.

Fibula: Smaller bone of the leg.

Fine: Having thin or slender jaws or tips.

Finger rings: Rings at the handling end of an instrument, used to control the jaws.

Fixation: To hold, suture or fasten in a fixed position, *e.g.*, fractured bone is stabilized in order for healing to take place; may be temporary or permanent.

Flaking: The tendency of some suture materials to release tiny particles of the suture in the wound.

Flash autoclave: An autoclave used in surgery to sterilize equipment quickly by steam under pressure.

Fracture: A break in the continuity of bone; see: compound fracture, simple fracture

Free tie: A term used by the surgeon when he or she requests a length of suture for legation.

French eye: A delicate needle whose double eye contains a spring.

Friable: Refers to any tissue that is easily torn.

General anaesthetic: An agent that produces both analgesia and unconsciousness.

Golding: The marking of instrument with a gold plating usually on the handles for easy identification; indicates the instrument has TC inserted or welded to its tips.

Goniometer device: Used to measure the flexibility and extension of the finger.

Gouge instrument: Used to scoop bone away from an area.

Hardening: Process by which steel is heated to very high temperatures in order to increase the metal's hardness or durability; also known as tempering.

Head: large rounded end of a bone.

Heavy: having broad jaws or tips.

Hemostasis : The control of bleeding.

Hemostat: An instrument used to clamp the blood vessel.

Hex size: Refers to the hexagonal tip of an instrument made to mate precisely, as in screwdrivers.

Humerus: The upper arm bone.

Identification and tracking: An electrochemical process is used in order to preserve the instrument surface; etching should never be performed on an instrument joint.

Implant Steel: Special grade of stainless steel used for manufacturing screws and plates for implantation in bone fixation procedures.

Inert: Refers to a quality of suture indicating that it causes little or no tissue reaction.

Infection: The invasion of healthy tissue by pathogenic micro-organisms.

Intervertebral: Between the vertebrae.

Intramedullary: Inside the medullary canal.

ISO: International Organization for Standardization; the organization which sets the manufacturing standards for certain surgical instruments, *e.g.*, internal fixation devices.

Jaws: Grasping or cutting tips of a ring-handled instrument.

Lamina: A thin layer of bone or membrane.

Laminectomy: Excision, or cutting away, of the posterior arch of a vertebrae.

Lap joint: Joint for a two-part instrument fastened in an overlapping fashion; used as an alternative to box locks.

Ligament: Tissue which serves to connect the ends of bones, binding them together or preventing movement.

Ligate: To tie a structure, such as a vessel.

Lumen: The cavity or channel within a tubular structure.

Malleable: Flexible, able to be bent.

Mallet: Hammerlike instrument used to apply force, e.g., to chisels and osteotomes.

Mating parts: Parts which interlock precisely, as in implant management instruments.

Medical practice acts: Laws that regulate the practice of physicians and surgeons.

Medullary canal: Bone marrow canal.

Meniscus: Crescent-shaped structure attached to the tibia (knee).

Metacarpal: Pertaining to the group of five long, thin bones which form the palm area of the hand.

Metatarsal: Pertaining to the group of five rod-shaped bones which form the arch of the foot.

Micro: Small, narrow or delicate.

Micrometer: Device used to take very fine measurements.

Microorganism: An organism that is visible only with the aid of a microscope. Causative agents of infections.

Milling: A stage in the manufacture of an instrument, in which the hot or cold forged blank is shaped, *e.g.*, to create the box lock.

Mycotic: Pertaining to mycosis, any disease caused by a fungus.

Necrosis: Death of areas of tissue or bone surrounded by healthy tissue; can be caused by excessive heating of bone during drilling.

Negligence: Acts of carelessness.

Neuroma: A tumor or new growth composed largely of nerve cells and fibers; a tumor which grows from a nerve.

Non-absorbable suture: A suture material that resists absorption by the body fluid.

Nonunion: failure of segments of broken bone to reunite.

Nurse practice acts: Laws that regulate the practice of nursing.

O.R.I.F.: Open Reduction, Internal Fixation.

Oblique: Inclined; sloping.

Obturator: Object which closes an entrance or cavity.

Occlude: To close or obstruct.

Olecranon: From the Greek, meaning "elbow".

Open reduction: Surgical procedure to reduce a fracture; open reduction may include the use of an internal fixation device.

Orthopedics: Area of medicine which deals with the treatment of disorders involving the structures of the body which enable movement, primarily the skeleton, joints, muscles and fascia.

Ostectomy: The removal of part or the entirety of a bone.

Osteosynthesis: Coined by Dr. Lambotte, refers to the process of surgical joining of bone fragments by internal fixation; now also used to refer to external fixation.

Osteotome: A chisel-like instrument, often used with a mallet to cut or sculpt bone, particularly cancellous bone.

Osteotomy: The surgical cutting or shaping of a bone; may include repositioning and/or controlled fracture.

Passivation: Electrochemical treatment of stainless steel to create passive layers.

Passive layers: Protective layers formed on stainless steel, the result of a high chromium content, which inhibit corrosion.

Patella: The knee cap.

Pathogenic: Disease-producing.

Pelvis: Bony structure which supports lower abdomen.

Periosteum: Connective tissue covering the external surface of a bone.

pH: Measurement for the acidity or alkalinity of a substance; distilled water has a neutral pH of 7.

Phalangeal: Refers to both the bones which form the toes or the bones which form the fingers and thumb; each group of phalanges includes 14 bones.

Pitting: Indentation on the surface of an instrument, caused by corrosion.

Purse-string: A type of suture technique whereby the suture is passed in a continuous circle around the lumen of a structure and tied in purse-string fashion.

QC handle: Quick-coupling handle, designed to mate quickly with QC working ends, as in some screwdrivers, taps and drills.

Radius: The bone of the forearm which rotates.

Ratchet: Locking mechanism located on the shank portion of an instrument.

Reduction: Restoration of a bone to its normal position; see: closed reduction and open reduction.

Reel: A round spool containing one long piece of suture from which the surgeon may cut any desired length of material for legation.

Resection: The operation of cutting out or removing a section or segment, *e.g.*, an organ.

Resident flora: Those bacteria that normally reside in or on the tissue of individuals.

Retention suture: Hoary non-absorbable sutures that are placed behind the main skin suture to give greater strength to the closure.

Retractor: Instrument used to grasp, retain or hold back tissue, organs or bone for surgical exposure.

Rongeur: A forcep used to cut or remove small pieces of bone and tissue.

Running stitch : A continuous strand of suture that is used to approximate tissue edges.

Saline: Solution of sodium chloride and distilled water; saline should not be used to clean instruments, as it may cause corrosion.

Sand-blasting: A surface treatment process by which tiny glass or sand beads are blasted under high pressure against the surface of a stainless steel instrument to achieve a homogeneous surface; used in cases where hand polishing is not possible or recommended.

Saw: A notched blade used for cutting.

Scissors: Cutting instrument with two shearing blades.

Screw: Lock a lap joint which is fixed with a screw, as with scissors.

Self-retaining: Capable of being placed in a fixed position, as in a self-retaining clamp.

Semi-box lock box: Lock which may be disassembled for cleaning.

Serrations: The small grooves seen on the edge or tips of an instrument; can be vertical, horizontal or diamond patterned.

Sesamoid: Small bone of the foot, usually found below the head of the first metatarsal bone (closest to the big toe).

Sesamoidectomy: The removal of a sesamoid bone.

Shanks: Midsection of a ring-handled instrument; site of ratchet.

Sharp: Implies a pointed tip, as in a rake retractor; frequent nickname for any sharp instrument, *e.g.*, scissors.

Simple fracture: A fracture which does not produce an open wound in the skin; also called "closed fracture".

Skeleton: The body's framework; in humans, the collective bones of the body.

Smooth: Without teeth; may be serrated, but does not have a projection to penetrate tissue.

Snare: An instrument with a wire loop used to remove a tissue growth by encircling it and removing the growth.

Soft tissue instruments: Basic instruments required for incision, subcutaneous tissue dissection and wound closure.

Spotting: Markings on an instrument caused by nonadhesive surface contaminents.

Staining: Markings on an instrument caused by semiadhesive surface contaminants; difficult to remove.

Stainless steel alloy of steels: The main metal is iron alloyed with chromium, carbon, manganese, silicon, etc.; chromium helps the steel to be rust resistant; other elements can be added so it can perform specific functions; used in the manufacture of most surgical instruments.

Steam sterilization: Process for the sterilization of instruments, using saturated steam at a set temperature and for a set time period; see: autoclave.

Sterilization: Process that removes all microbes, including spores, to render instruments safe for use; usually achieved with a steam or gas process; see: autoclave, steam sterilization.

Sternum: The breast bone.

Strabismus: Deviation of the eye which prevents both eyes from looking at an object at the same time; cross-eye.

Suction: Tip a hollow, tubelike instrument which is attached to a vacuum for suction.

Synovectomy: Removal of a synovial membrane.

Synovium: Membrane which lines the inside of a joint.

Tarsal: Pertaining to the group of seven bones which form the ankle and heel.

TC inserts: Tungsten carbide inserts, soldered or welded into the jaw of an instrument to provide extra durability; TC inserts may also be replaced, extending the life of an instrument.

Teeth: Small notches or projections used to grasp tissue and prevent the instrument from slipping.

Tempering: See hardening.

Tenaculum: Hooklike instrument used to seize and hold tissue.

Tendon: A cord of tissue which connects muscle to bone.

Tenotomy: Dissection or cutting of tendon or muscle, as in hand, foot and eye surgery.

Thoracic: Pertaining to the chest.

Tibia: Shin bone.

Tissue: A group of cells which are specialized to perform a particular function.

Tolerance: The allowable amount of variation in the dimensions of an instrument.

Tonometer: Instrument used to measure the tension or pressure of the eyeball or the blood pressure within blood vessels.

Tool steel: Type of steel generally used for machine-shop tools, used in the manufacture of some instruments.

Tooling machines: Tools, fixtures and other devices which aid in the manufacture of instruments.

Toothed: See: teeth.

Traumatic having a crushing or biting effect on tissue.

Traumatize: To wound or damage.

Trochanter: Either of two bony processes, or protuberances, of the upper shaft of the femur which serves in the attachment of muscle.

Tungsten carbide: Alloy used in the manufacture of inserts for instrument tips; harder than stainless steel; tungsten has the highest melting point of all metals.

Ulna: The inner and larger bone of the forearm.

Ultrasonic cleaner: Mechanical cleaner which makes use of sound waves (known as cavitation) to clean instruments; used before lubrication and sterilization.

REFERENCES

1. **Nancymarie, Howard Fortunato: Berry and Kohn's** Operating Room Technique; Ninth edition, Mosby, 2000.

2. **Ministry of Health,** Disease Prevention and Control Department: Infection Prevention Guidelines for Healthcare.

3. **Brunner and Suddarth's:** Textbook of Medical – Surgical Nursing; Eighth Edition; Lippincott, Philadelphia, 1996.

LIST OF ABBREVIATIONS AND ACRONYMS

ACP : Anaesthesia Care Providers

AIDS : Acquired Immune Deficiency Syndrome

AORN : Association of peri-Operative Registered Nurses

B & S : Brown and Sharp

CDC : Center for Disease Control and Prevention

Cm : Centimeter

CPR : Cardiopulmonary Resuscitation

ECG : Electrocardiography

EO/ETO : Ethylene Oxide

ESU : Electrosurgical Unit

FDA : Food and Drug Administration

Fig. : Figure

HBV : Hepatitis B-Virus

HCV : Hepatitis C-Virus

HIV : Human Immunodeficiency Virus

ICU : Intensive Care Unit

I.D. : Identification

i.e. : that is

IM : Intramuscular

IP : Infection Prevention

IV : Intravenous

MH : Malignant Hyper Thermia

Ml : Milliliter

N/A : No Activity/ Not Applicable

NATN : National Association of Theatre Nurses

N.B. : Nota Bene

NRL : Natural Rubber Latex

OR : Operating Room

OSHA : Occupational Safety and Health Administration

PPE : Personal Protective Equipment

RR : Recovery Room

TB : Tuberculosis

U.S.P. : United States Pharmacopoeia

WHO : World Health Organization

Multiple Choice Questions

1. How many phases include in peri-operative care?
   A. 1
   B. 2
   C. 3
   D. 4

2. Which phase is not included in peri-operative care?
   A. Pre-operative
   B. Intra-operative
   C. Post-operative
   D. None of these

3. What is the Means of Restricted Area in operation theatre?
   A. Area in which only sterile things happen
   B. Area in which only unsterile things happen
   C. Area in which no activity happen
   D. Area in which only doctors do activity

4. What is the role of OTA?
   A. Help to provide anaesthesia
   B. Help in scrubing
   C. Help in surgery
   D. All of them

5. Which is not included in patient care?
   A. Surgeon
   B. Anaesthesia provider
   C. Nurse and cleaner
   D. Company man

6. OT floor is made by as:
   A. Smooth and non-porous material
   B. Hard and porous material
   C. Does not matter
   D. Slippery matter

7. OT floor made by smooth and non-porous material:
   A. To prevent infection
   B. To prevent injury
   C. To prevent smooth running of equipment
   D. All of them

8. How many area divided into OT Area?
   A. 3
   B. 2
   C. 1
   D. 5

9. Which is not an Operation Theatre Area?
   A. Unrestricted Area
   B. Restricted Area
   C. Semi-restricted Area
   D. None of these

10. What is the meaning of WHO?
    A. World Health Organization
    B. World Home Organization
    C. Wild Health Organization
    D. None of these

11. What is the purpose of hand hygiene?
    A. Mechanically removed soil and debris from skin
    B. Clinically removed soil and debris from skin
    C. Both A and B
    D. None of these

12. What is the meaning of hand antisepsis?
    A. Mechanically removed soil and debris from skin
    B. Remove the transient and resident flora on the hands
    C. Both A and B
    D. None of these

13. What is Hand rub?
A. Vigorously rubbing the hand by antiseptic lotion
B. Vigorously rubbing the hand without antiseptic lotion
C. Normal handwashing
D. None of these

14. What is hand rubbing time?
A. 15 – 30 seconds
B. 30 – 45 seconds
C. 5 sec
D. ½ hrs

15. Which is not a basic rule of sterility?
A. Unsterile person touches the sterile things
B. Sterile person is in touch of sterile things
C. Sterile each member face each other
D. Sterile tables are sterile only at table's height

16. What is OSHA?
A. Occupational safety and health administers
B. Occupational source and health administers
C. Occupational ship and health administers
D. None of them

17. What is universal precaution?
A. Prevent by barrier technique
B. Prevent by only gown
C. Prevent by only gloves
D. Prevent by both gown and gloves

18. What is steam sterilizer?
A. Prevent things sterilized by only steam
B. Prevent things sterilized by antiseptic
C. Prevent things sterilized by both A & B
D. None of these

19. Who propounded Germ Theory?
A. Louis Pasteur   B. Joseph Lester
C. Robert Koch   D. Ronald

20. Who is the Father of Morden Surgery?
A. Louis Pasteur   B. Joseph Lester
C. Robert Koch   D. Ronald

21. What is Surgical attire?
A. Provide such as masks, gowns, gloves
B. Provide only gloves
C. Provide only gown
D. None of them

22. Which is not a component of Attire?
A. Body cover
B. Shoe cover, apron
C. Gloves and gown
D. Watch

23. What is meaning of transient organism?
A. Acquired by direct contact
B. Acquired by indirect contact
C. Self acquired
D. Both A and C

24. What is meaning of Resident Organism?
A. Found below the skin surface
B. Found anywhere
C. Found only in deeper tissue
D. Both A and C

25. Which is not a gown and gloves wearing technique?
A. Open technique   B. Mixed technique
C. Closed technique D. None of them

26. Which is not a Scrub equipment?
A. Brushes   B. Soaps
C. Nail cleaners   D. None of them

27. Why we remove jewellery before surgical scrub?
A. To prevent infection
B. For fear of loss
C. Both A and B
D. None of them

28. How many methods are for gowning?
A. Gowning self   B. Gowning another
C. Both A and B   D. None of these

29. Definition of sterilization is:
A. the process by which all pathogenic and non-pathogenic microorganism killed
B. the process by which all only pathogenic microorganism killed
C. the process by which all non-pathogenic microorganisms killed
D. All the above

30. Which is not a chemical method of sterilization?
A. EO gas
B. Glutaraldehyde 2%
C. Formaldehyde 8%
D. Heat

31. What is temperature and pressure, and time in autoclaver?
A. 25 to 30 minutes at 121 – 132°C and 121 pa
B. 10 min – 12P-132°C and 121pa
C. 30 – 35 minutes and 121-132°C
D. Does not depend

32. Which is sterilize by Dry heat?
A. Oils, sharps
B. Sponges/bandages
C. All of them
D. Only sharps

33. What is the temperature of Dry heat?
A. 170°C for 60 min
B. 170°C to 80 min
C. 160°C for 60 min
D. Does not depend

34. What is ETO?
A. Ethylene tri oxide
B. Ethylene tetra oxide
C. Ether tri oxide
D. None of them

35. Which factor is not influence the effectiveness of disinfectant?
A. Nature of items
B. Contact time
C. Concentration of solution
D. None of them

36. High level of disinfection include
A. Virus
B. Bacteria
C. TB
D. All of them

37. What is the formula of making concentration?

A. $\left[\dfrac{\%\ \text{concentrate}}{\%\ \text{dilute}}\right] - 1$

B. $\left[\dfrac{\%\ \text{concentrate}}{\%\ \text{solvent}}\right] - 2$

C. Both A and B

D. $\left[\dfrac{\%\ \text{concentrate}}{\%\ \text{dilute}}\right] - 3$

38. How many people minimum requires for patient positioning?
A. 4
B. 3
C. 2
D. 1

39. At the time of giving Anaesthesia in general, which position given?
A. Supine
B. Prone
C. Standing
D. Does not depend

40. At the time of giving Spinal Anaesthesia, which position given?
A. Lateral
B. Sitting
C. Standing
D. Both A and B

41. At the time of spine surgery, which position given?
A. Prone
B. Lateral
C. Supine
D. Standing

42. Which position given in eye surgeries?
A. Supine
B. Prone
C. Lateral
D. Standing

43. Mostly this position given in abdominal surgeries:
A. Supine
B. Prone
C. Lateral
D. Standing

44. Which position given in vaginal delivery?
A. Lithotomy position
B. Supine
C. Standing position
D. Does not depend

45. Which position is given in orthopaedics surgery?
A. Supine
B. Lateral
C. Prone
D. All of them

46. Which position given in Head/Neck surgeries?
A. Demanded by surgeon
B. As prone
C. As supine
D. Lithotomy position

47. Which is the most important things for position of patient?
A. Surgical site is most clear
B. Patient skin integrity
C. Joint mobility
D. All of them

48. What is patient drapping?
A. Before surgical incusion, site of incision is covered by clothes
B. Around the surgical site covered by water impermeable drape
C. Patient covered by drape
D. None of them

49. How many types of drapes available in market?
A. Plastic drape
B. Cloth drape
C. Water impermeable drape
D. All of these

50. What is Anaesthesia?
A. Absence of sensation
B. Absence of concurrences
C. Absence of heart rate
D. Absence of respiration

51. Which of the following food would be avoided from alcoholic client?
A. Milk
B. Orange juice
C. Tea
D. Regular coffee

52. A Neuromuscular Agent is administered before ECT therapy. What will you observe?
A. Nausea
B. Vomiting
C. Seizures
D. Dizziness

53. Exposure to sunlight helps a person to improve his health because:
A. The ultraviolet ray converts skin oil into vitamin D
B. Body resistance power increases
C. The pigment cells increase
D. None of these

54. As technician is caring for a client with a newly applied plaster cast. How should the technician touch and move the wet cast?
A. Use of palms of the hands
B. Use of finger tips only
C. Use of a towel sling
D. Touch the cast only on the petal at the edges

55. A young child adult is discharged to home with crutch which exercise should the nurse teach the client in order to strengths the hand muscle for crutch walking?
A. Pushing the buttocks up off the matters
B. Pulling the body up
C. Raising the legs
D. Sequeezing the rubber ball

56. When informed consent is obtained for surgery who must explain the surgical procedure to the client?
A. Physician
B. Nurse
C. Anaesthologist
D. Operation Theate Nurse

57. An adult is to have abdominal surgery this morning immediately pre-operatively we ensure that:
A. is comfortable
B. has an empty bowel
C. practice coughing
D. voids

58. A young man hand an emergency appendectomy for a rupture appendix and is in post-anaesthesia which position given?
A. Right sims position
B. Dorsal
C. Trendelenburg position
D. Semi-sitting position

59. Which is not a type of anaesthesia?
A. Local anaesthesia
B. Caudal
C. Spinal
D. None of them

60. Which is not a local infiltration?
A. Lignocaine
B. Lignocaine with Adrenaline

C. Morphine
D. None of them

61. Regional Anaesthesia includes?
A. Caudal   B. Epidural
C. Spinal   D. All of them

62. Which is not a method of given general Anaesthesia?
A. Inhalation   B. Intra venous
C. Intra muscular   D. None of them

63. Which is not an inhalation agent?
A. Nitrous oxide   B. Haloathene
C. Isofurane   D. None of them

64. Which is not a intra venous agent?
A. Midazolam
B. Glyco and Fentanyl
C. Ketamine
D. None of them

65. Why diazepam is given?
A. Anticanvulsants
B. Antihypertensive
C. Antientire
D. Antipyretic

66. Lidocaine is used for?
A. Local anaesthesia
B. General anaesthesia
C. Both A and B
D. None of these

67. Which is not an adverse reaction to local anaesthesia?
A. Patient may become very talkative
B. Patient may become very anxious
C. Patient may become very hypertensive
D. None of them

68. Which is not a muscle relaxants?
A. Vecuronium bromide
B. Fentanyl
C. Sufenatatil
D. None of them

69. What is the role of Acetaminophen drug?
A. Mild analgesia
B. Mild antipyretic
C. Antiseptic
D. Both A and B

70. Which ointment is commonly used in operation theatre for eye care?
A. Neosporin   B. Neomycin
C. Both A and B   D. None of them

71. Which is an anticoagulants drugs?
A. Heparin   B. Erythromycin
C. Protamine   D. Both A and B

72. Above Elbow slab related to:
A. Forearm fracture
B. Elbow Fracture
C. Wrist Fracture
D. All of them

73. What is PoP?
A. Plaster of Paris
B. Plaster of Pyrenia
C. Both A and B
D. None of these

74. Above knee cast is related to:
A. Knee fracture   B. Elbow fracture
C. Hand fracture   D. None of these

75. Volar slab related to:
A. Finger fracture   B. Wrist fracture
C. Hip fracture   D. Knee fracture

76. What is the meaning of legatee?
A. A structure to clamp to vessel
B. A structure to open to vessel
C. A structure both clamp and legatee to vessel
D. None of these

77. What is OTA?
A. Operation Theatre Assistance
B. Operation Theatre Awareness
C. Operation Theatre All
D. None of these

78. What composition is in hand source?
A. Propylene Glycol 52% w/w
B. Sodium salicylate 46% w/w
C. Sodium lauryl sulphate 4% w/w
D. All of them

79. What composition is in sterillium?
A. 2-propanol
B. 1-propanol
C. ethyl-hexadecyl-dimethyl, Ammonium-ethyl sulphate
D. All of them

80. What is the role of Tourniquet?
A. To stop the blood supply in surgical site
B. To stop the blood supply in throughout body
C. To increase blood supply
D. None of them

81. What is Tincture Benzoin?
A. Alcohol base
B. Ether base
C. Aldhehyde base
D. None of them

82. Lignocaine jelly is used as a:
A. General anaesthesia
B. Local anaesthesia
C. Spinal anaesthesia
D. None of these

83. Lignocaine jelly usually is used in anaesthesia for:
A. High vascular tissue
B. Low vascular tissue
C. Soft tissue
D. None of them

84. Who is Father of Surgery?
A. Sushruta   B. Aristotle
C. Louis Pasteur   D. None of these

ANSWERS

1	2	3	4	5	6	7	8	9	10
C	D	A	D	D	A	D	A	D	A

11	12	13	14	15	16	17	18	19	20
C	B	A	A	A	A	A	A	A	B

21	22	23	24	25	26	27	28	29	30
A	D	A	D	B	D	A	C	A	D

31	32	33	34	35	36	37	38	39	40
A	C	A	A	D	D	A	A	A	D

41	42	43	44	45	46	47	48	49	50
A	A	A	A	D	A	D	B	D	A

51	52	53	54	55	56	57	58	59	60
D	D	A	A	D	B	B	B	D	C

61	62	63	64	65	66	67	68	69	70
D	D	D	D	A	A	D	D	D	C

71	72	73	74	75	76	77	78	79	80
D	A	A	A	A	A	A	D	D	A

81	82	83	84
A	B	A	A

GENERAL SCIENCE

1. Which of the following is *not* a physical change?
    A. Boiling of water to give water vapour
    B. Melting of ice to give liquid water
    C. Dissolution of salt in water
    D. Combustion of Liquefied Petroleum Gas (LPG)

2. Which of the following gives the correct increasing order or acidic strength?
    A. Water < Acetic acid < Hydrochloric acid
    B. Water < Hydrochloric acid < Acetic acid
    C. Acetic acid < Water < Hydrochloric acid
    D. Hydrochloric acid < Water < Acetic acid

3. The ability of metals to be drawn into thin wires is known as
    A. ductility   B. malleability
    C. sonorosity   D. conductivity

4. Gunmetal contains
    A. Cu = 60%, Sn = 40%
    B. Cu = 80%, Sn = 20%
    C. Cu = 70%, Sn = 30%
    D. Cu = 90%, Sn = 10%

5. MRI stands for
    A. Magnets Resonant Imaging
    B. Magnetic Resonance Imaging
    C. Magnetic Radar Imaging
    D. Magnet Radial Imaging

6. What is the maximum resistance which can be made using five resistors each of $\frac{1}{5}\Omega$?
    A. $\frac{1}{5}\Omega$ B. $10\ \Omega$
    C. $5\ \Omega$ D. $1\ \Omega$

7. Which of the following is *not* associated with growth of plants?
    A. Auxins   B. Gibberellins
    C. Cytokinins   D. Abscisic acid

8. In a neuron, conversion of electrical signal to a chemical signal occurs at/in
    A. cell body   B. axonal end
    C. dendritic end   D. axon

9. Drinking alcohol is very harmful and it ruins the health. 'Drinking alcohol' stands for
    A. drinking methyl alcohol
    B. drinking ethyl alcohol
    C. drinking propyl alcohol
    D. drinking isopropyl alcohol

10. Which of the following elements does *not* lose an electron easily?
    A. Mg   B. Na
    C. K   D. Ca

11. Length of pollen tube depends on the distance between
    A. pollen grain and upper surface of stigma
    B. pollen grain on upper surface of stigma and ovule
    C. pollen grain in anther and upper surface of stigma
    D. upper surface of stigma and lower part of style

12. Gonorrhoea is caused by a bacterium called
    A. *Neisseria gonorrhoeae*
    B. *Treponema pallidum*
    C. *Lactobacillus*
    D. *Streptococcus*

13. Which of the following is *not* a natural resource?
    A. Soil   B. Water
    C. Electricity   D. Air

14. Which of the following is a 'biodiversity hot spot'?
    A. Rivers   B. Forests
    C. Deserts   D. Oceans

15. Depletion of ozone is mainly due to
    A. chlorofluorocarbon
    B. carbon monoxide
    C. methane
    D. pesticides

16. Which group of organisms are *not* constituents of a food chain?
A. Grass, lion, rabbit
B. Plankton, man, fish, grasshopper
C. Wolf, grass, snake, tiger
D. Frog, snake, eagle, grass, grasshopper

17. Red light is used for danger signal as
A. it has higher wavelength
B. it can travel large distance
C. it scatters the least
D. it scatters the longest

18. Twinkling of stars is due to atmospheric
A. dispersion of light by water droplets
B. refraction of light by different layers of varying refractive indices
C. scattering of light by dust particles
D. internal reflection of light by clouds

19. The chief function of lymph nodes in the body is to
A. produce red blood cells
B. collect and destroy pathogens
C. produce a hormone
D. destroy the old and worn out red blood cells

20. Which is the first enzyme to mix food in the digestive tract?
A. Pepsin   B. Cellulase
C. Amylase   D. Trypsin

21. What happens, when zinc metal is dipped in copper sulphate solution?
A. the solution becomes colourless and reddish brown copper metal gets deposited
B. no reaction takes place
C. the solution becomes green and copper metal gets deposited
D. the solution remains blue and copper metal gets deposited

22. In binary fission of a cell:
A. Cytoplasm and nucleus divide at the same time.
B. The division of nucleus is followed by the division of cytoplasm.
C. The division of cytoplasm is followed by the division of nucleus.
D. The cytoplasm and nucleus do not divide.

23. When a cell is kept in a hypotonic solution then water moves:
A. into the cell
B. out of the cell
C. no movement of water takes place
D. none of these is correct

24. The isomers of C_6H_{14} are:
A. 4   B. 5
C. 6   D. 3

25. Which among the following diseases is ***not*** sexually transmitted?
A. Syphillis   B. Hepatitis
C. HIV-AIDS   D. Gonorrhoea

26. A full length image of a distant tall building can definitely be seen by using:
A. a concave mirror
B. a convex mirror
C. a plane mirror
D. both concave as well as plane mirror

27. The human eye forms the image of an object at its:
A. cornea   B. iris
C. pupil   D. retina

28. Which one of the following is an artificial ecosystem?
A. Pond   B. Crop field
C. Lake   D. Forest

29. Extensive plantation of trees to increase forest cover is known as:
A. Agro-forestry   B. Social forestry
C. Afforestation   D. Deforestation

30. Which of the following is an exothermic process?
A. Reaction of water with quicklime
B. Dilution of an acid
C. Evaporation of water
D. Sublimation of Camphor

31. Which among the following is ***not*** a base?
A. NaOH   B. KOH
C. NH_4OH D. C_2H_5OH

32. Blood bank of the body is:
A. spleen   B. heart
C. liver   D. bone marrow

33. Electrical resistivity of a given metallic wire depends upon:
A. its length   B. its thickness
C. its shape   D. nature of material

34. Growth of the plant or plant parts towards the earth is called:
A. phototropism   B. hydrotropism
C. thigmotropism   D. geotropism

35. The unit of electric power may also be expressed as:
A. Volt ampere   B. Kilowatt hour
C. Watt second   D. Joule second

36. Biogas is a better fuel as it has:
A. 75% methane
B. higher calorific value
C. residual manure
D. all of these

37. Which of the following is different from the other three?
A. petroleum   B. coal
C. natural gas   D. geothermal

38. The centre for controlling body temperature is:
A. Hypothalamus
B. Cerebellum
C. Central nervous system
D. Cerebrum

39. The ability of metals to be drawn into thin wire is known as:
A. ductility   B. malleability
C. sonorousity   D. conductivity

40. Galvanisation is a method of protecting iron from rusting by coating with a thin layer of:
A. Galium   B. Aluminium
C. Zinc   D. Silver

41. Which of the following represents a chemical change?
A. Evaporation of alcohol
B. Sublimation of iodine
C. Heating of a platinum wire in a bunsen flame
D. Heating of mercuric oxide powder

42. The chemical used as a 'fixer' in photography is:
A. Sodium sulphate
B. Sodium thiosulphate
C. Ammonium persulphate
D. Borax

43. Which of the following in solid state is known as dry ice?
A. Ammonia   B. Nitrogen
C. Carbon dioxide   D. Hydrogen

44. The tape of tape recorder is coated with:
A. Copper sulphate
B. Mercury
C. Ferromagnetic powder
D. Zinc oxide

45. During dehydration, what is slightly lost actually?
A. Sodium Chloride
B. Potassium Chloride
C. Calcium Chloride
D. Calcium Sulphate

46. Rayon is chemically a:
A. cellulose   B. amylase
C. glucose   D. pectin

47. The process of obtaining salt from sea water is called:
A. Evaporation   B. Sublimation
C. Crystallization   D. Distillation

48. The silver surface of thermos flask prevents the transfer of heat by:
A. Convection   B. Conduction
C. Radiation   D. Reflection

49. The hardness of water can be removed by:
A. Zeeolite   B. Sodium Silicate
C. Boiling   D. None of these

50. The most common acid found in the nature is:
A. Citric acid
B. Lactic acid
C. Acetic acid
D. Hydrochloric acid

51. The speed of light will be minimum, while passing through:
A. Vacuum   B. Glass
C. Air   D. Water

52. The final image produced by a simple microscope is:

A. Virtual and erect   B. Erect and real
C. Real and inverted   D. Virtual and real

53. The change of ice into water is a/an:
A. Chemical change   B. Physical change
C. Atomic change   D. Electrical change

54. An air bubble in water will act like a:
A. Convex lens   B. Convex mirror
C. Concave lens   D. Concave mirror

55. Plants absorb water from the soil by:
A. Gravitational process
B. Capillary process
C. Hygroscopic process
D. None of these

56. The main endocrine gland present in human body is:
A. Pituitary gland   B. Adrenal gland
C. Thyroid gland   D. Pancreas gland

57. In human body, the water quantity is about:
A. 20%   B. 100%
C. 80%   D. 65%

58. Which of the following chemicals is used for preserving fruit juices in India?
A. Sodium hydroxide
B. Potassium nitrate
C. Ammonium sulphate
D. Sodium benzoate

59. The atmospheric layer nearest to earth is:
A. Stratosphere   B. Troposphere
C. Ionosphere   D. Mesosphere

60. Which of the following gases does not pollute air?
A. Sulphur dioxide
B. Nitrogen oxide
C. Carbon dioxide
D. Carbon monoxide

61. Refractive index of a medium—
A. has no unit
B. has an unit
C. has a value equal to 1 or less than one
D. has a value less than one

62. Three primary colours are—
A. red, green and yellow
B. red, green and blue
C. green, yellow and orange
D. violet, yellow and red

63. Which physical quantity is represented by Coulomb per second ?
A. charge   B. electric current
C. potential difference   D. resistance

64. A wire of resistance 2 ohms is bent in the form of a closed circle. The effective resistance between the two points at the end of any diameter of the circle is ;
A. 0.5 ohm   B. 1 ohms
C. 2 ohms   D. 4 ohms

65. The frequency of an alternating current whose direction changes after every 0.01 second is :
A. 1 Hz   B. 2 Hz
C. 50 Hz   D. 100 Hz

66. How much solar energy will be received by 1 m^2 area in one hour ? (Solar constant = 1.4 kW/m^2)—
A. 1400×1 J   B. 1400×60 J
C. $1.40 \times 60 \times 60$ J   D. $1400 \times 60 \times 60$ J

67. Speed of light is maximum in the following (out of 4 given media)—
A. water   B. glass
C. diamond   D. air

68. Average age of red blood cells (RBC) is approximately :
A. one day   B. 30 days
C. 60 days   D. 120 days

69. On adding lime juice to distilled water its pH—
A. remains unchanged
B. becomes 7
C. becomes less than 7
D. becomes more than 7

70. The valency shown by an element having atomic number 12 is—
A. 1   B. 2
C. 4   D. 6

71. Chemical formula for baking soda is—
A. NaOH   B. $NaHCO_3$
C. $Ca(OH)_2$ D. Na_2CO_3

72. Pure gold is :
A. 1 carat gold   B. 18 carat gold
C. 22 carat gold   D. 24 carat gold

73. The agency responsible for running space research programmes in India is—
A. IRS   B. UGC
C. ISRO   D. IARI

74. The first Indian satellite sent to space was named—
A. Rohini   B. Dhruv
C. Aryabhatt   D. Sputnik

75. In Hydrilla plant stomata are present—
A. On stem
B. On leaves
C. On both stem and leaves
D. No where as they are absent in Hydrilla

76. The excretory unit of kidney is—
A. neuron   B. hormone
C. photon   D. nephron

77. The author of the book 'The origin of species' is—
A. Charles Darwin   B. Lamarck
C. J.D. Watson   D. Weismann

78. The time period of geosynchronous satellite is—
A. One hour
B. Twelve Hours
C. Twenty-four hours
D. One year

79. If we draw a V-I graph for a conductor (V = P.D. across the conductor and I = current flowing through it) it will be as shown in figure.

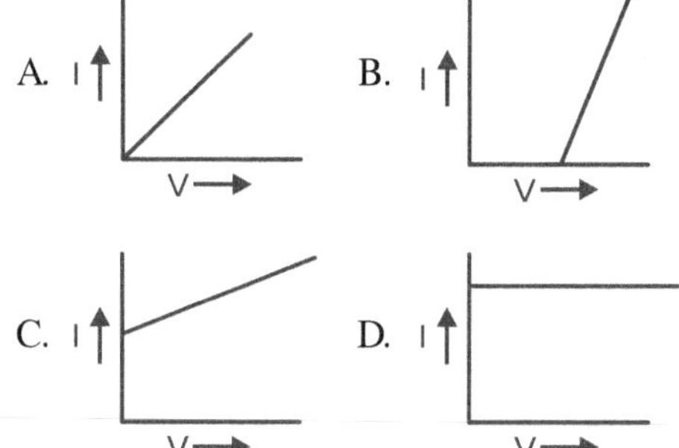

80. AIDS is caused by—
A. Fungus   B. Virus
C. Bacterium   D. Malnutrition

81. Lime water contains—
A. Calcium carbonate
B. Calcium hydroxide
C. Calcium bicarbonate
D. Sodium sulphate

82. Which of the following represents a chemical change?
A. Evaporation of alcohol
B. Sublimation of iodine
C. Heating of a platinum wire in bunsen flame
D. Heating of mercuric oxide powder

83. Pencillin is obtained from—
A. Algae fungi   B. Fungi
C. Synthetics   D. None of these

84. Isotopes differ in—
A. Number of electrons
B. Number of protons
C. Number of neutrons
D. Protons and neutrons

85. The drug most widely used to relieve pain is—
A. Paracetamol   B. Aspirin
C. Morphine   D. Nimusulide

86. A person climbing a hill bends forward in order to—
A. Avoid slipping   B. Increase speed
C. Reduce fatigue   D. Increase stability

87. The technique used to transmit audio signals in television broadcast is—
A. Amplitude modulation
B. Frequency modulation
C. Pulse code modulation
D. Time division multiplexing

88. Which of the following is the most elastic?
A. carbon   B. rubber
C. glass   D. paper

89. Energy is measured in the same unit as that of—
A. Work   B. Power
C. Momentum   D. Inertia

90. A device used in converting a.c. current into d.c. is called—
A. Transformer   B. Rectifier
C. Induction coil   D. Dynamo

91. Which of the following blood group is universal recipient?

A. A   B. B
C. AB   D. O

92. Which of the following is most important for digestion?
A. Proteins   B. Milk
C. Fat   D. Vitamins

93. The human skull consists of—
A. 22 bones   B. 14 bones
C. 8 bones   D. None of these

94. The first life of earth came—
A. In water   B. On land
C. In air   D. On mountains

95. DNA is concentrated in the—
A. Microsome   B. Nucleus
C. Protoplasm   D. Chromatin

96. Why is 28th February is observed as National Science Day?
A. Birth of Dr. Bhabha
B. First Indian atomic explosion
C. The world came to know about Raman Effect
D. A SLVD-1 launched

97. Which of the following is neither an element nor a compound?
A. Air   B. Water
C. Glucose   D. Gold

98. Which of the following gas does not pollute air?
A. Carbon dioxide
B. Carbon monoxide
C. Nitrogen oxide
D. Sulphur dioxide

99. The main atmospheric gas responsible for green house effect is—
A. Nitrogen   B. Oxygen
C. Ozone   D. Carbon dioxide

100. The atmospheric layer nearest to earth is—
A. Stratosphere   B. Troposphere
C. Ionosphere   D. Mesosphere

101. Jaundice is due to the infection of—
A. Brain   B. Liver
C. Kidney   D. Spleen

102. In a normal person average rate of heart beat is—
A. 82   B. 92
C. 72   D. 98

103. EEG is used for the observation of which part of the body?
A. Heart   B. Lungs
C. Brain   D. Muscles

104. Colour of cows milk is light yellow due to—
A. Zenthophil   B. Riboflevin
C. Ribulos   D. Kerotin

105. Which of the following is infectious—
A. Diabetes   B. Diphtheria
C. Arthritis   D. Cancer

106. Which of the following is less in Anaemia?
A. Haemoglobin   B. Collagen
C. Highoglobin   D. Myosin

107. Which of the following disease spreads through air?
A. Plague   B. Typhoid
C. Tuberculosis   D. Cholera

108. Cereals are rich sources of—
A. Starch   B. Glucose
C. Fructose   D. Maltose

109. Aspirin is the ordinary name of—
A. Salicylic Acid
B. Salicylate
C. Methyl Salicylate
D. Acetylsalicylic Acid

110. Reason of small Pox is—
A. Rubiola Virus   B. Variola Virus
C. Varicela   D. Mixovirus

111. Carbon Monoxide is an inflammable gas. Which of the following is also an inflammable gas—
A. Helium   B. Nitrogen
C. Oxygen   D. Hydrogen

112. In the Aerobic Respiration which of the following is needed—
A. Heat   B. Water
C. Oxygen   D. Sunlight

113. Which of the following does not produce Hydrogen in reaction with water—
A. Potassium   B. Cadmium
C. Sodium   D. Lithium

114. Ozone contains—
A. Only Oxygen

B. Oxygen and Nitrogen
C. Hydrogen and Carbon
D. Oxygen and Carbon

115. Which of the following liquid is of low density—
A. Fresh water   B. Salt water
C. Petrol   D. Mercury

116. Which of the following theory is used to produce low-temperature—
A. Super conductivity
B. Joule-Kelvin effect
C. Thermoelectric effect
D. Adiabatic demagnetisation

117. Photoelectric cell transforms—
A. Mechanical energy into electrical energy
B. Heat energy into mechanical energy
C. Light energy into chemical energy
D. Light energy into electrical energy

118. Two stones of different masses if fallen down from the peak of the building—
A. small stone reaches before on the ground
B. big stone reaches before on the ground
C. both stones reach together on the ground
D. it depends on the construction of stones

119. Pulsar are—
A. stars moving towards earth
B. stars moving far away to earth
C. fastest moving stars
D. stars having high temperature

120. Ozone hole in the atmosphere is situated at—
A. Above the Arctic ocean
B. Above the Antarctica
C. Above the India
D. Above the Alaska

121. Clothes do not dry quickly on a rainy day because on a rainy day—
A. Humidity is high
B. Humidity is low
C. Temperature becomes high
D. Atmospheric pressure rises

122. Joule is the unit of—
A. Force   B. Power
C. Energy   D. Pressure

123. The audible range of hearing for average human beings is—
A. 20 Hz to 20 KHz   B. 2 Hz to 20 Hz
C. 2 Hz to 20 KHz   D. 2 KHz to 20 KHz

124. Tritium is an—
A. Isobar of Hydrogen
B. Isotope of Hydrogen
C. Isobar of Helium
D. Isotope of Helium

125. Which of the following ions helps in the opening and closing of stomata?
A. Na^+ B. K^+
C. Ca^{++} D. None of the above

126. Which of the following does not have plus (+) or minus (–) signs marked on it?
A. Resistor   B. Ammeter
C. Voltmeter   D. Battery

127. Photosynthesis is a—
A. Catabolic process
B. Anabolic process
C. Amphibolic process
D. All of these

128. If a mirror forms an erect but diminished image of an object placed anywhere in front of it, is a—
A. Concave Mirror
B. Plane Mirror
C. Convex Mirror
D. Concave and Convex Mirror (both)

129. The instrument to measure atmospheric pressure is called—
A. Pyrometer   B. Thermopile
C. Barometer   D. Manometer

130. Orange colour of the setting sun is due to—
A. Reflection of light
B. Diffusion of light
C. Scattering of light
D. Polarisation of light

131. What is the final colour of blue litmus when a dilute solution of NaOH is added to it?
A. Red   B. Pink
C. Orange   D. Blue

132. Pick the odd one out—
  A. Fermentation
  B. Aerobic Respiration
  C. Anaerobic Respiration
  D. Breathing

133. Hypotonic solution as compared to Hypertonic solution has—
  A. More solute
  B. Less solute
  C. Same solute
  D. Nothing can be said about the amount of solute

134. Volt is the unit of—
  A. Charge   B. Current
  C. Resistance   D. Potential difference

135. Two resistors having resistances of 1 ohm and 2 ohms respectively are connected in series with a battery. The current through the 2 ohms resistor is 2 amperes. The current through the 1 ohm resistor will be—
  A. 0.5 amp   B. 1 amp
  C. 2 amp   D. 4 amp

136. The addition of which one of the following will decrease the pH value of water?
  A. Caustic Soda   B. Baking soda
  C. Salt   D. Hydrochloric acid

137. The branch of science that deals with tumours is—
  A. Osteology   B. Anatomy
  C. Oncology   D. Urology

138. Pneumonia is a disease associated with—
  A. Liver   B. Lungs
  C. Gums   D. Kidney

139. 'Decibel' is a measure of—
  A. Time   B. Distance
  C. Intensity of sound D. Energy

140. Which of the following have the highest frequency?
  A. Heat waves   B. Sound waves
  C. Ultraviolet rays D. Gamma rays

141. Which of the following colours has the shortest wavelength?
  A. Red   B. Orange
  C. Yellow   D. Violet

142. In a diesel engine, the fuel is ignited by:
  A. a spark plug
  B. liquid oxygen
  C. the heat generated when air is compressed in the cylinder
  D. vaporization under partial vacuum

143. How many moons does the Pluto have?
  A. None   B. One
  C. Two   D. Six

144. The weight of a body on the moon is:
  A. 1/5th of its weight on earth
  B. 1/6th of its weight on earth
  C. 1/7th of its weight on earth
  D. 1/100th of its weight on earth

145. The scientific study of the action of chemicals upon living beings is called:
  A. Pharmacy   B. Pharmacognosy
  C. Pharmacology   D. Biochemistry

146. In the manufacturing of match stick, which of the following is used?
  A. Potassium
  B. Sodium
  C. White phosphorous
  D. Red phosphorous

147. What did Fleming discover?
  A. Vitamin A   B. Vaccines
  C. Sulphonamides   D. Penicillin

148. The substance present inside a fluorescent tube which emits light is:
  A. Nitrogen   B. Mercury vapour
  C. Sodium cyanide D. Air

149. The biological process by which changes occur in genes is known as:
  A. Adaptation   B. Evolution
  C. Natural selection D. Mutation

150. Agronomy is the study of:
  A. behaviour of agricultural animals
  B. field crop production and soils
  C. names of agricultural plants
  D. all of these

151. Cold-blooded animals are those animals whose:
  A. blood is cold
  B. blood is blue, not red

C. body temperature varies with that of the surroundings

D. body temperature is always constant

152. What is the technical term for fish farming?
A. Aviculture B. Sericulture
C. Pisciculture D. Zooculutre

153. The vision defect of eyes as a result of which a person is unable to see distant objects clearly, is called:
A. Hypermetropia B. Long sightedness
C. Astigmatism D. Myopia

154. Which of the following diseases is caused by amoeba?
A. Paralysis B. Cholera
C. Dysentery D. Typhoid fever

155. The wind blowing from the land towards the sea during the night is known as:
A. Ordinary breeze B. Sea breeze
C. Land breeze D. Cold breeze

156. Dots are placed on dice in such a fashion that the sum of dots on any two opposite sides is always:
A. 9 B. 7
C. 6 D. 8

157. If the earth did not spin:
A. we would have no seasons
B. half of earth would always be in sunlight
C. there would be no summer in the northern hemisphere
D. all of the above

158. The most abundant element in the earth's crust is:
A. Oxygen B. Silicon
C. Aluminium D. Iron

159. The term Green Revolution refers to:
A. increase in milk production
B. increase in vegetable production
C. involvement of Dr. Green in agriculture
D. increase in crop production

160. When a person donates blood, approximately how much of his/her blood is taken?
A. 250 – 300 ml B. 1000 ml
C. 1 – 2 litre D. 50 ml

161. Which of the following are *not* electromagnetic waves?
A. Infra-red waves
B. Laser waves
C. Ultrasonic waves
D. Microwaves

162. Domestic electric meters record the consumption of electricity in
A. Volts B. Amperes
C. Watts D. Ohms

163. Which of the following is used for time keeping in an atomic clock?
A. Cesium B. Helium
C. Plutonium D. Nitrogen

164. When an aeroplane takes off, air pressure on the
A. top surface of its wings is less than the air pressure on the bottom surface
B. top surface of its wings is more than the air pressure on the bottom surface
C. top and bottom surfaces of its wings is exactly equal
D. wings is zero

165. The pH value of pure water is
A. 7 B. 0
C. 14 D. –1.0

166. The substance which readily hardens, when mixed with water is
A. Plaster of Paris B. Granite
C. Lime D. Silica

167. The gas commonly used for cooling in a domestic refrigerator is
A. Carbon monoxide
B. Propane and butane mixture
C. Helium
D. Neon

168. Stainless steel is basically formed by the combination of iron and
A. Chromium B. Carbon
C. Manganese D. Cobalt

169. The tube which connects the mouth to the stomach is known as
A. oesophagus B. trachea
C. larynx D. intestine

170. DNA molecules have the shape of
A. a string of beads
B. a double helix
C. a cylindrical mass
D. None of the above

171. Which portion of the egg contains cholesterol?
A. Egg white   B. Shell of the egg
C. Egg yolk   D. All parts equally

172. Aspirin is the common name of
A. salicylic acid
B. salicylate
C. acetyl salicylic acid
D. methyl salicylate

173. During galvanization, the substance which is coated on the surface of iron to protect it from rusting is
A. galium   B. aluminium
C. tin   D. zinc

174. The intensity of earthquakes is measured by
A. Algal scale   B. Crescograph
C. Ritcher scale   D. Cryptograph

175. Solar eclipse occurs when
A. earth comes between sun and moon
B. moon is at right angle to the earth
C. moon comes between sun and earth
D. sun comes between moon and earth

176. Which of the following are fossil fuels?
A. Coal and biogas
B. Petroleum and biogas
C. Biogas and coal gas
D. Coal, petroleum and natural gas

177. Clouds of intersteller matter found in space is known as
A. galaxies   B. constellations
C. quasars   D. nebula

178. The mass of a material divided by its volume is its
A. gravity   B. relative density
C. specific gravity   D. density

179. The removal of a piece of tissue from a living person for examination is known as
A. autopsy   B. necropsy
C. biopsy   D. histology

180. If a red coloured rose is examined in green light, it will appear
A. white   B. black
C. grey   D. brown

181. The carriers of genetic information are
A. Proteins
B. Lipids and Minerals
C. Nucleic acids
D. Carbohydrates

182. Wind velocity is measured by
A. Anemometer   B. Hydrometer
C. Barometer   D. Hygrometer

183. The causative organism of rabies disease is
A. Bacterium   B. Virus
C. Fungus   D. Algae

184. Which of the following is *not* a plant product?
A. Cotton   B. Lac
C. Jute   D. Sugar

185. Which vitamin in blood plays an important role in clotting?
A. Vitamin A   B. Vitamin D
C. Vitamin E   D. Vitamin K

186. The digestion of starch in the diet starts in the
A. Liver   B. Stomach
C. Intestine   D. Mouth

187. Vitamin C is chemically known as
A. Ascorbic acid   B. Aspartic acid
C. Citric acid   D. Tartaric acid

188. Which one of the following radiations is most penetrating?
A. X-rays   B. Alpha rays
C. Beta rays   D. Gamma rays

189. An atom with an electronic configuration 2, 8, 8 has a valency of
A. -1 B. Zero
C. $+1$ D. $+8$

190. Which of the following elements forms the largest number of compounds?
A. Hydrogen   B. Oxygen
C. Silicon   D. Carbon

191. Which of the following gases has lowest density?

A. Argon   B. Helium
C. Oxygen   D. Nitrogen

192. In the formation of Ni^{++}, nickel
A. gains two electrons
B. loses two electrons
C. loses two protons
D. gains two protons

193. If 8.0 g of a metallic oxide on decomposition gives 1·6 g oxygen, what is the equivalent weight of the metal?
A. 8   B. 16
C. 32   D. 64

194. Sphere A attracts Sphere B as well as Sphere C. Sphere B repels Sphere C. If Sphere C is negatively charged it can be concluded that
A. Sphere A is positively charged
B. Sphere A is netagively charged
C. Sphere A is either positively charged or is uncharged
D. Sphere A is either negatively charged or is uncharged

195. The domestic consumption of electricity is calculated in
A. Joules   B. Watts
C. Kilowatt/hour   D. Kilowatt hours

196. The apparent depth of a pond full of water whose real depth is 8 metres will be
A. 2 metres   B. 3 metres
C. 6 metres   D. 8 metres

197. The rays which are *not* deflected by electric or magnetic field are
A. Alpha rays   B. Beta rays
C. Gamma rays   D. Positive rays

198. A metal surface ejects electrons when hit by green light but no electron is ejected when hit by yellow light. The electrons will be ejected when the surface is hit by
A. Blue light   B. Red light
C. Infra-red light   D. Heat rays

199. Two coils have a combined resistance of 12 ohms when connected in series and 3 ohms when connected in parallel. The respective resistances are
A. 4 ohms, 8 ohms   B. 6 ohms, 6 ohms
C. 9 ohms, 3 ohms   D. 10 ohms, 2 ohms

200. A hole is drilled through the earth along its diameter and a stone is dropped into it. At the centre of the earth, the stone possesses
A. Acceleration   B. Kinetic energy
C. Potential energy   D. no energy

ANSWERS

1	2	3	4	5	6	7	8	9	10
D	A	A	D	B	D	D	B	B	A
11	**12**	**13**	**14**	**15**	**16**	**17**	**18**	**19**	**20**
C	A	C	B	A	C	C	B	B	C
21	**22**	**23**	**24**	**25**	**26**	**27**	**28**	**29**	**30**
A	A	B	B	B	B	D	A	C	A
31	**32**	**33**	**34**	**35**	**36**	**37**	**38**	**39**	**40**
D	A	D	D	B	D	D	A	A	C
41	**42**	**43**	**44**	**45**	**46**	**47**	**48**	**49**	**50**
D	B	C	C	A	A	A	B	C	A
51	**52**	**53**	**54**	**55**	**56**	**57**	**58**	**59**	**60**
A	D	B	C	B	D	D	D	B	C
61	**62**	**63**	**64**	**65**	**66**	**67**	**68**	**69**	**70**
C	B	A	B	C	C	D	D	C	B

71	72	73	74	75	76	77	78	79	80
B	D	C	C	D	D	A	C	A	B

81	82	83	84	85	86	87	88	89	90
A	C	B	C	B	D	B	A	A	D

91	92	93	94	95	96	97	98	99	100
B	D	B	A	B	C	A	C	D	B

101	102	103	104	105	106	107	108	109	110
B	C	C	D	B	A	A	A	D	B

111	112	113	114	115	116	117	118	119	120
D	C	B	A	C	A	D	C	C	B

121	122	123	124	125	126	127	128	129	130
A	C	A	B	B	A	C	C	C	C

131	132	133	134	135	136	137	138	139	140
D	A	B	D	C	D	C	B	C	D

141	142	143	144	145	146	147	148	149	150
D	A	A	B	C	D	D	A	D	B

151	152	153	154	155	156	157	158	159	160
C	C	D	C	C	B	D	C	D	A

161	162	163	164	165	166	167	168	169	170
C	C	A	A	A	A	D	A	A	B

171	172	173	174	175	176	177	178	179	180
C	C	D	C	C	D	D	D	C	B

181	182	183	184	185	186	187	188	189	190
C	A	A	B	D	D	A	D	B	D

191	192	193	194	195	196	197	198	199	200
B	B	B	A	C	A	C	A	C	D

GENERAL KNOWLEDGE

1. Which unit of valuation is known as 'Paper Gold'?
   A. Petrodollar   B. SDR
   C. Eurodollar   D. GDR

2. The coastline that borders the state of Kerala, is known as
   A. Konkan Coast   B. Malabar Coast
   C. Coromandel Coast D. Canara Coast

3. Who is the founder of World Economic Forum?
   A. Klaus Schwab
   B. John Kenneth Galbraith
   C. Robert Zoellick
   D. Paul Krugman

4. The concept of sustainable development relates to
   A. Consumption levels
   B. Exhaustible levels
   C. Social equity
   D. None of these

5. Article-17 of the Constitution provides for
   A. Equality before law
   B. Equality of opportunity in matters of public employment
   C. Abolition of titles
   D. Abolition of untouchability

6. Where did the practice of 'Shadow Cabinet' originate?
   A. USA   B. Great Britain
   C. Italy   D. France

7. The Indian Citizenship Act was passed in
   A. 1950   B. 1952
   C. 1955   D. 1960

8. Saka Era which starts from 78 AD represents
   A. Kanishka's reign
   B. Prosperity of Harsha
   C. Shivaji's reign
   D. Chandragupta's reign

9. The foundation stone of the Gateway of India was laid in
   A. 1911   B. 1927
   C. 1857   D. 1947

10. Almatti Dam is located on which of the following rivers?
    A. Godavari   B. Kaveri
    C. Krishna   D. Mahanadi

11. Which of the following are the youngest mountains of India?
    A. Aravallis   B. Himalayas
    C. Nilgiris   D. Vindhyachal

12. Gresham's law in Economics relates to
    A. Supply and demand
    B. Circulation of currency
    C. Consumption of supply
    D. Distribution of goods and services

13. Revealed Preference Theory was propounded by
    A. Adam Smith   B. Marshall
    C. P.A. Samuelson D. J.S. Mill

14. The Indian Independence League was set up by
    A. Rash Behari Bose
    B. S.M. Joshi
    C. Aruna Asaf Ali
    D. Jai Prakash Narayan

15. The description of Caste System is found in
    A. Rig Veda   B. Sam Veda
    C. Yajur Veda   D. None of these

16. The capital of Pallavas was
    A. Arcot   B. Kanchi
    C. Malkhed   D. Banaras

17. In early medieval India, what did the term 'Jital' refer to?
    A. Weight   B. Diet
    C. Coin   D. Game

18. Which of the following is *not* a Kharif crop?
    A. Rice   B. Groundnut
    C. Maize   D. Barley

19. Which one of the following is a landlocked sea?
    A. Timor Sea   B. Arafura Sea
    C. Greenland Sea   D. Aral Sea

20. Which of the following straits separates Europe from Africa?
    A. Bering   B. Dover
    C. Gibraltar   D. Malacca

21. Who was the Viceroy of India when Rowlatt Act passed?
    A. Hardings II   B. Chelmsford
    C. Simon   D. Minto II

22. The Vindhyan System of Rocks is important for the production of:
    A. precious stones and building material
    B. iron ore and managanese
    C. bauxite and mica
    D. copper and uranium

23. Which of the following acts gave representation to Indians for the first time in the legislature?
    A. Indian Council Act 1909
    B. Indian Council Act 1919
    C. Govt. of India Act 1935
    D. Govt. of India Act 1942

24. Which document was developed mentioning Samudragupta's Achievements?
    A. Kalinga Edict
    B. Hathigumpha Edict
    C. Indica
    D. Allahabad Prasasti

25. Which of the following Articles of the Directive Principles of State Policy deals with the promotion of International Peace and Security?
    A. Article 51   B. Article 48A
    C. Article 43A   D. Article 41

26. In which of the following matters does Lok Sabha has supremacy?
    A. Railway Budget   B. Defence Budget
    C. Foreign Affairs   D. Financial Bill

27. As per existing law what is the minimum per day wages paid to a worker from unorganised sector in India?
    A. ₹ 50   B. ₹ 75
    C. ₹ 100   D. ₹ 125

28. Who is the first law officer of the Govt. of India?
    A. The Chief Justice of India
    B. Union Law Minister
    C. Attorney General of India
    D. Law Secretary

29. Many a times we see in financial Journals/Bulletins a term M_3, what does the term M_3 mean?
    A. Currency in circulation on a particular day
    B. Total value of the foreign Exchange on a particular day
    C. Total value of Export Credit on a given date
    D. Total value of the tax collected in a year

30. Many a times we read in the newspapers that RBI has changed or revised a particular ratio/rate by a few base points. What is meant by base point?
    A. Ten per cent of one hundredth point
    B. One hundred of 1%
    C. One hundred of 10%
    D. Ten per cent of 1000

31. Nagarjuna Sagar Dam is built across the river:
    A. Cauvery   B. Krishna
    C. Narmada   D. Godavari

32. Firoz Shah founded many cities, which of the following was not built by him?
    A. Jaunpur   B. Fatehpur Sikri
    C. Hisar   D. Fatehabad

33. The Red Sea is an example of a:
    A. folded structure   B. faulted structure
    C. lava structure   D. residual structure

34. Isochrones are lines joining places with equal:
    A. longitude
    B. travelling time from a point
    C. rainfall
    D. frost

35. The pepper plant is a:
A. tree
B. vine
C. shrub
D. small herb

36. Which kind of power accounts for the largest share of power generation in India?
A. Hydro Electricity
B. Thermal
C. Nuclear
D. Solar

37. An image of dancing girl on the coins was found from:
A. Kalibangan
B. Harappa
C. Mohenjodara
D. Ropar

38. The Italian traveller who gave a very praise worthy account of the Vijaynagar Empire was:
A. Barbosa
B. Marco Polo
C. Nicolo Conti
D. Tome Pires

39. Iqtas were:
A. hereditary assignments
B. the personal property of the nobles
C. generally transferable revenue assignments
D. orders passed by kings and queens

40. The number of languages listed in 8th schedule of the Constitution of India is:
A. 15
B. 18
C. 22
D. 14

41. Mohen-jo-daro is situated at:
A. Punjab
B. Gujarat
C. Sindh
D. Uttar Pradesh

42. The first governor general of the independent India was:
A. C. Rajagopalachari
B. Dr. Rajendra Prasad
C. Lord Mountbatten
D. Dr. B.R. Ambedkar

43. Grand Trunk road was made by:
A. Chandragupta Maurya
B. Shahjahan
C. Shershah Suri
D. Lord Dalhousi

44. Large production of jute is at the delta of river:
A. Damodar
B. Sindh
C. Ganga
D. Satluj

45. Which state of India is largest in area?
A. Uttar Pradesh
B. Madhya Pradesh
C. Assam
D. West Bengal

46. The highest mountain peak in India is:
A. Kanchenjunga
B. Mount Everest
C. Nanda Devi
D. Annapurna

47. Largest river in India is:
A. Ganga
B. Kaveri
C. Brahmaputra
D. Godavari

48. Father of local self governance is:
A. Lord Ripen
B. Lord Curzon
C. Lord Minto
D. Lord Dalhousi

49. Section 370 of constitution of India gives special status to which state?
A. Sikkim
B. Nagaland
C. Arunachal Pradesh
D. Jammu and Kashmir

50. The members of Rajya Sabha are elected:
A. Directly by people
B. By members of parliament
C. By members of legislative assembly
D. By the president of India

51. Who constitutes the Finance Commission?
A. Lok Sabha
B. President
C. Rajya Sabha
D. Finance Minister

52. Who is the Chairperson of Planning Commission?
A. Prime Minister
B. Home Minister
C. President
D. Finance Minister

53. Panchayati Raj system was first introduced in the state of:
A. Bihar
B. West Bengal
C. Andhra Pradesh
D. Rajasthan

54. The capital of Sikkim is:
A. Gangtok
B. Shillong
C. Imphal
D. Dispur

55. The state with highest population density is:
A. Uttar Pradesh
B. Arunachal Pradesh
C. West Bengal
D. Bihar

56. The smallest state of India is:
A. Haryana
B. Punjab
C. Bihar
D. Goa

57. The state with highest number of tribes is:
A. West Bengal   B. Bihar
C. Jharkhand   D. Madhya Pradesh

58. Who said 'Go back to Vedas'?
A. Dayanand Saraswati
B. Vivekananda
C. Swami Shradhananda
D. Ram Krishna Paramhansa

59. Who initiated 'Deen-e-elahi?
A. Jahangir   B. Shershah
C. Aurangzeb   D. Akbar

60. Coal production is highest in the state of:
A. Jharkhand   B. Odisha
C. Bihar   D. Madhya Pradesh

61. The most important kingdom in Deccan and Central India after the Maurya has that of the :
A. Satvahans   B. Cholas
C. Pallavas   D. Pandyan

62. Alberuni came to India in:
A. 9th Century AD   B. 10th Century AD
C. 11th Century AD   D. 12th Century AD

63. The planning commission was set up in:
A. March 1950   B. March 1951
C. April 1951   D. April 1952

64. What is the consequence of the writ of Habeas Corpus?
A. The person under detention is set free
B. The public servant is restrained from taking any action
C. The officer not competent to take certain action is told not to go ahead with the action
D. More information is sought from the lower court

65. Which of the following river is called 'Biological Desert' due to heavy population?
A. Brahmaputra   B. Ganga
C. Damodar   D. Yamuna

66. Which of the following foreign kings was not a contemporary of Ashoka?
A. Antiochos Theos
B. Magas
C. Ptolemy Philadelphos
D. Daurius II

67. Who is remembered as the pioneer of Economic Nationalism?
A. Bipin Chandar Pal
B. Gokhale
C. R. C. Dutt
D. Madan Mohan Malviya

68. Lapps inhabit—
A. East Africa
B. European Steppes
C. South American grasslands
D. European Tundra

69. India's national game is :
A. Football   B. Cricket
C. Tennis   D. Hockey

70. Who is one of the propounders of the binary star theories?
A. Laplace   B. Kant
C. La-Pichon   D. Jeffreys

71. In which state was Panchayat Raj first introduced?
A. Gujarat   B. Rajasthan
C. Bihar   D. Andhra Pradesh

72. The electoral system of India is largely based on the pattern of :
A. Britain   B. France
C. USA   D. None of these

73. Monoculture is a typical characteristic of :
A. Shifting cultivation
B. Subsistence farming
C. Specialized horticulture
D. Commercial grain farming

74. Horse latitudes is the term applied to the :
A. $0° – 5°$ N and S latitudes
B. Polar circles
C. $30° – 40°$ N and S latitudes
D. $40° – 60°$ N and S latitudes

75. In the vedic period goghna refers to :
A. One who gifts cattle
B. One who slaughters cattle
C. A guest
D. The bridegroom

76. 'Half an hour discussion' can be raised in the house of parliament after giving notice to the :
A. Presiding officer of the house

B. The Secretary - General of the house
C. The Secretary of the department of parliamentary affairs
D. Concerned minister

77. Fiscal policy is connected with :
A. Exports and imports
B. Public revenue and Expenditure
C. Issue of currency
D. Population control

78. Who of the following was the first speaker of Lok Sabha?
A. Hukum Singh
B. G.S. Dhilon
C. G.V. Mavalankar
D. Ananthaswayanam Ayenger

79. Who amongst the following was impeached in England for Acts Committed as Governor General of India?
A. Wellesley
B. Cavendish Bentick
C. Cornwallis
D. Warren Hastings

80. Which year is known as 'Year of the Great divide' with regard to population growth in India?
A. 1921
B. 1947
C. 1951
D. None of these

81. The planet nearest to sun is—
A. Mars
B. Mercury
C. Venus
D. Neptune

82. Thimpu is the capital of—
A. Sikkim
B. Meghalaya
C. Bhutan
D. Mizoram

83. Railways was introduced in India in the year—
A. 1901
B. 1883
C. 1853
D. 1908

84. Kolar gold mines are in the state of—
A. Madhya Pradesh
B. Karnataka
C. Tamil Nadu
D. Orissa

85. The novel 'Devdas' is written by—
A. Sharatchandra Chatterjee
B. Rabindranath Tagore
C. Prem Chandra
D. Bankimchandra Chattopadhyaya

86. Ballarpur is known for—
A. Writing paper
B. Coal mines
C. Fertilizers
D. Cement plant

87. India is a 'republic' because—
A. Democratic rule exists here
B. Its head of state (country) is elected
C. Its constitution is written
D. All of the above

88. The duration of 'Zero hour' in Lok Sabha is—
A. 15 minutes
B. Half-an-hour
C. One hour
D. Not-specified

89. Lakshadweep is a group of .... islands.
A. 22
B. 27
C. 32
D. 35

90. The Sikh Guru who faught against the Mughals was—
A. Guru Nanak Dev
B. Guru Arjun Dev
C. Guru Tegh Bahadur
D. Guru Gobind Singh

91. How many spokes are there in our national emblem 'Ashok Chakra'?
A. 12
B. 15
C. 20
D. 24

92. The first Indian film in colour was—
A. Jhansi ki Rani
B. Aan
C. Sairandhri
D. Ramrajya

93. British shifted their capital from Calcutta to Delhi in—
A. 1905
B. 1909
C. 1911
D. 1914

94. Who gave the slogan 'Jai Hind'?
A. Mahatma Gandhi
B. Pandit Jawaharlal Nehru
C. Subhash Chandra Bose
D. Bhagat Singh

95. The number of seats allotted to different states in the Lok Sabha is determined on the basis of state's—
A. Population
B. Size
C. Resources
D. Location

96. The Andes Mountain range is in—
A. Europe
B. North America
C. Africa
D. South America

97. Konkan Railway runs between—
A. Mumbai-Manglore
B. Mumbai-Goa

C. Manglore-Trivandrum
D. Goa-Kanyakumari

98. The Indus Valley people had trade relations with—
A. Groooo
B. Egypt
C. Ceylon
D. Mesopotamia

99. Which of the following is not an essential elements of the state?
A. Territory
B. Society
C. Government
D. Population

100. When a bill is referred to a joint meeting of both the houses of the Indian Parliament, it has to be passed by—
A. A simple majority
B. Three-fourth majority
C. Two-third majority
D. Absolute majority of total membership

101. Three bigha corridor combines—
A. India and Pakistan
B. India and China
C. Bangladesh and Pakistan
D. Bangladesh and India

102. Who built the Vijay Stambh in Chittor?
A. Maharana Pratap
B. Rana Sangram Singh
C. Rana Kumbha
D. Rana Ratan Singh

103. Which religious book was called as 'mother' by Gandhiji?
A. Ramayana
B. The New Testament
C. Bhagvatgeeta
D. Kuran Sharif

104. Tihari water electrical complex is situated on the bank of river—
A. Alaknanda
B. Mandakini
C. Dhauli Ganga
D. Bhagirathi

105. The person who had made the design of Rashtrapati Bhawan was—
A. Adward Stone
B. Le Kaburje
C. Advin Lutians
D. Tarun Dutta

106. 'Quit India' movement 1942 was commenced in the month of—
A. January
B. March
C. August
D. December

107. Match the following—
Group-I
(a) Keshav Chandra Sen
(b) Dayanand Saraswati
(c) Atmaram Pandurang
(d) Syed Ahmed Khan
Group-II
1. Prarthana Samaj
2. Brahma Samaj
3. Aligarh Movement
4. Arya Samaj

	(a)	(b)	(c)	(d)
A.	4	1	3	2
B.	1	4	2	3
C.	2	4	1	3
D.	3	2	4	1

108. Who was the first British President of Indian National Congress?
A. George Yule
B. William Vederbern
C. A.O. Hume
D. Henery Coton

109. Which person is known as 'Grand old man of India'?
A. Bal Gangadhar Tilak
B. Dada Bhai Nauroji
C. Moti Lal Nehru
D. Lala Lajpat Rai

110. Who wrote the 'Akbarnama'?
A. Akbar
B. Birbal
C. Abul Fajal
D. Bhagwan Das

111. In India, Panchayati Raj System was introduced—
A. In 1950
B. In 1945
C. In 1959
D. In 1962

112. The person who was elected twice as the Vice-President was—
A. Dr. S. Radhakrishnan
B. Shri R. Venkat Raman
C. Dr. Shankar Dayal Sharma
D. Shri V. V. Giri

113. By which amendment of Indian constitution two words - Socialist and Secular was added in the Preamble?

A. 28   B. 40
C. 42   D. 52

114. Indian constitution adhered to—
A. 26 January, 1950
B. 26 January, 1952
C. 15 August, 1948
D. 26 November, 1949

115. Who was the first lady governor of a state in free India?
A. Smt. Sarojini Naidu
B. Smt. Sucheta Kriplani
C. Smt. Indira Gandhi
D. Smt. Vijaya Luxmi Pandit

116. Name the parliamentary committee which scrutinizes the report of Comptroller and Auditor General.
A. Estimates Committee
B. Select Committee
C. Public Accounts Committee
D. None of these

117. Which of the following shows the joining line of the places where rainfall are equal?
A. Iisohips   B. Iisohelienj
C. Isobar   D. Isohytes

118. Equator line is—
A. the line which joins the North and South pole
B. the imaginary line which moves exactly in the centre of the earth of North and South Pole
C. A girdle around Saturn (planet)
D. An axis of rotation of earth

119. Which is not correct when the interest rate is high in the economic system?
A. saving increases
B. process of lend decreases
C. cost of production increases
D. resultant of capital increases

120. Labour Intensive Technique will be selected in—
A. In labour surplus economy
B. In capital surplus economy
C. In developed economy
D. In developing economy

121. The Treaty of Sreerangapattanam was between Tipu Sultan and—
A. Cornwallis   B. Clive
C. Warren Hastings D. Wellesley

122. The famous Besnagar Pillar Inscription of century 150 BC refers to the great theistic cult of—
A. Panchika and Hariti B. Pashupatis
C. Krishna-Vasudeva D. Shakti

123. What is the water hyacinth?
A. A weed
B. A medicinal plant
C. A decorative plant
D. A highly sought after plant

124. To which of the following bills must the President accord his sanction without sending it back for recommendations?
A. Ordinary bills
B. Finance bills
C. Bills passed by both the houses of Parliament
D. Bills seeking amendment to the Constitution

125. The amendment procedure of the Indian Constitution has been modelled on the constitutional pattern of—
A. Canada   B. USA
C. Switzerland   D. South Africa

126. Indian Railways tied up with which of the following to launch a co-branded card and traveller loyalty card to tap the huge railway passengers market?
A. BoB cards   B. Citibank card
C. SBI card   D. None of these

127. Which bank advertises itself as the world's local bank?
A. Citibank   B. HSBC
C. ICICI Bank   D. ABN Amro

128. In which state is Silent Valley located?
A. Tamil Nadu
B. Kerala
C. Assam (Asom)
D. Arunachal Pradesh

129. Which of the following is not a promotional and motivational measure suggested in the National Population Policy 2000?

A. Reward Panchayat and Zila Parishad for promoting small family norm
B. Incentive to adopt two child norm
C. Couples below poverty line will be given health insurance plans
D. Banning abortion facilities (looking at female infanticides)

130. Who said, "HANOZ DELHI DOOR AST"?
A. Nizamuddin Aulia B. Farid
C. Nasiruddin D. None of these

131. In which of the following constitutional documents did the British Government for the first time, officially lay down as the goal of constitutional development in India, not only dominion status, but also responsible Government?
A. Indian Council Act, 1892
B. Indian Council Act, 1909
C. Government of India Act, 1919
D. Government of India Act, 1935

132. In which state is chromite abundantly found?
A. Maharashtra B. Madhya Pradesh
C. Orissa D. Karnataka

133. For what is the Manas Sanctuary in Assam known?
A. Bear B. Tiger
C. Wild ass D. Birds

134. The Rajya Sabha can take initiative in—
A. Censuring a Central Minister
B. Creating a new All India Service
C. Considering Money Bills
D. Appointing Judges

135. Which of the following provides the largest part of the demand for loanable funds in India?
A. Hire purchase borrowers
B. Private house purchasers
C. Corporate businesses
D. Farmers

136. Who amongst the following was impeached in England for acts committed as Governor General of India?
A. Wellesley
B. Cavendish Bentinck
C. Cornwallis
D. Warren Hastings

137. The National Stock Exchange of India (NSEI) was inaugurated in—
A. July 1992 B. July 1993
C. July 1994 D. July 1995

138. One of the major towns of the Godavari region in the Satavahana kingdom was—
A. Pratishthana B. Arikamedu
C. Kokkhai D. Maski

139. In the Islamic (Mughal) buildings that came up in India, the elements of decoration did not include—
A. Calligraphy
B. Depiction of living beings
C. Geometry
D. Foliage

140. Jaya is the name of a high yielding variety of—
A. Wheat B. Rice
C. Bajra D. Cotton

141. What is the rank of India in the 2004 Index of Economic Freedom, published by the Heritage Foundation and the Wall Street Journal?
A. 84 B. 71
C. 121 D. 90

142. Who was the Governor-General when the 1857 revolt broke out?
A. Dalhousie B. Canning
C. Curzon D. Lawrence

143. The Twelfth Finance Commission has recommended to bring down the revenue deficit of the Centre and the State to zero by
A. 2005-2006 B. 2006-2007
C. 2007-2008 D. 2008-2009

144. In Union Budget 2005, the finance minister introduced a new tax called FBT. What is the full name of the term FBT?
A. Fiscal Benefit Tax
B. Fringe Benefit Tax
C. Fixed Benefit Tax
D. None of these

145. Fawazil was
A. extra payment made to the nobles
B. excess amount paid to the Exchequer by the Iqtedar

C.   revenue assigned in lieu of salary
D.   none of these

146. Which one of the following is *not* a statutory body?
 A.   The Election Commission
 B.   The Union Public Service Commission
 C.   The Planning Commission
 D.   The Finance Commission

147. Which of the following countries is *not* a member of Mercosur?
 A.   Brazil   B.   Paraguay
 C.   Peru   D.   Chile

148. Which theory makes the use of Jigsaw fit in its support?
 A.   Tidal Hypothesis
 B.   Tetrahydral Hypothesis
 C.   Cycle of Erosion
 D.   Continental Drift Theory

149. Where is the famous Tuscarora dweep located?
 A.   Near USA
 B.   Off Japan
 C.   Off Lakshadweep
 D.   Near the Australian coast

150. In which of the following countries has there been the highest rise in overall level of skilled unemployed during 2000-2002?
 A.   India   B.   China
 C.   France   D.   USA

151. The Rigveda consists of
 A.   1028 hymns   B.   1000 hymns
 C.   2028 hymns   D.   1038 hymns

152. Blizzards are characteristic of .... region.
 A.   Equatorial   B.   Tropical
 C.   Antarctic   D.   Temperate

153. Which of the following Harappan sites are located in Uttar Pradesh?
 A.   Kalibangan   B.   Banawali
 C.   Alamgirpur   D.   Sutkagen-dor

154. The Prime Minister Manmohan Singh has constituted a task force to prepare a long term plan for the social and economic development of:
 A.   Tamil Nadu

B.   Manipur
C.   Jammu and Kashmir
D.   Uttarakhand

155. How many islands make up Hong Kong?
 A.   235   B.   245
 C.   205   D.   206

156. Commonwealth Bank belongs to which country?
 A.   Australia   B.   New Zealand
 C.   United Kingdom   D.   Philippines

157. What does NIFE refer to?
 A.   A crop
 B.   An instrument
 C.   A marine organism
 D.   A type of rock

158. Who started the Madras Labour Union in 1918?
 A.   Kanji Dwarkadas and Umar Sobhani
 B.   G. Ramanjulu Naidu and G.C. Chetti
 C.   T.K. Murlidhar and H.B. Mahaduvle
 D.   C.K. Annadurai and K.T. Ramchandar

159. Which of the following rivers is called Biological Desert due to heavy population?
 A.   Brahmaputra   B.   Ganga
 C.   Damodar   D.   Yamuna

160. Where do Bhagirathi and Alaknanda join to form Ganga?
 A.   Karna Prayag   B.   Dev Prayag
 C.   Rudra Prayag   D.   Gangotri

161. What is the name of the man who discovered that the Monsoon winds blow regularly across the Arabian Sea in summer?
 A.   Ptolemy   B.   Hippalus
 C.   Pliny   D.   Megasthenes

162. Who is remembered as the pioneer of Economic Nationalism?
 A.   Bipin Chandar Paul
 B.   Gokhale
 C.   R.C. Dutt
 D.   Madan Mohan Malviya

163. In the Allahabad district in 1929, at a time of the world-wide economic depression, 'no tax' campaign on behalf of peasants was led by

A. Jawahar Lal Nehru
B. Sahajanand Saraswati
C. M.N. Roy
D. P.C. Joshi

164. 'My own belief is that the Congress is tottering, and one of my great ambition is to assist it to a peaceful death.' Who said it?
A. Winston Churchill
B. Lord Canning
C. Lord Curzon
D. Mohammad Ali Jinnah

165. Aurangzeb was a scholar of
A. Poetry
B. Muslim theology and jurisprudence
C. Persian literature
D. Persian warfare

166. Who is connected with the 'Blue Water' Policy?
A. Albuquerque
B. Dupleix
C. De Almeida
D. Robert Clive

167. Who was called the 'Rapheal of the East'?
A. Bihzad of Herat
B. Sayyad Ali
C. Khwaja Abdus Samad
D. Farrukh Beg

168. Fiscal policy is connected with
A. Exports and imports
B. Public revenue and expenditure
C. Issue of currency
D. Population control

169. The expression 'The Union of States' used in the Constitution has been taken from the Constitution of
A. Canada
B. USA
C. USSR
D. Germany

170. Which one of the following statements correctly describes 'a hung Parliament'?
A. A Parliament in which no party has a clear majority
B. The Prime Minister has resigned but the Parliament is not dissolved
C. The Parliament lacks the quorum to conduct business
D. A lame duck Parliament

171. For what is Philadelphia well known?
A. Ship building
B. Dairy industries
C. Locomotives
D. Silk textiles

172. Which state is the leading producer of thorium?
A. Kerala
B. Bihar
C. Orissa
D. Madhya Pradesh

173. Who are believed to be the oldest inhabitants of India?
A. Mediterraneans
B. Negritoes
C. Nordics
D. Mongoloids

174. Most of the precipitation in India is
A. Cyclonic
B. Convectional
C. Orographic
D. Stormy

175. Who put forth the nebular hypothesis explaining the origin of the earth?
A. Wegener
B. Laplace
C. Kant
D. Jeans and Jeffreys

176. Leeds is well known for
A. Cotton textiles
B. Iron smelting
C. Films
D. Woollen textiles

177. The plan holiday refers to the period
A. 1965-68
B. 1966-69
C. 1967-70
D. 1978-80

178. Which of the following is the Indian contribution to Parliamentary procedures?
A. Zero session
B. Cut-motion
C. Adjournment motion
D. Guillotine

179. The only European country which did *not* prohibit or impose heavy duties on the import of Indian cotton goods was
A. Germany
B. France
C. Holland
D. Italy

180. Regarding the earliest surviving Buddhist art, what *cannot* be said to have particularly appealed to the Europeans is that it was
A. Non-symbolic
B. Anecdotal
C. Iconographic
D. Narrative

181. Budha preached his first sermon at
A. Lumbini
B. Sarnath
C. Varanasi
D. Gaya

182. Meghasthenes visited India during the reign of
A. Harsha

B. Ashoka
C. Chandra Gupta Maurya
D. Kanishka

183. The *Ain-e-Akbari* was written by
A. Farishta
B. Badauni
C. Birbal
D. Abul Fazal

184. Ibn Batuta visited India during the reign of
A. Balban
B. Ala-uddin Khilji
C. Razia
D. Muhammad Bin Tughlaq

185. The Third Battle of Panipat was fought between
A. Britishers and Marathas
B. Marathas and Rajputs
C. Afghans and Sikhs
D. Marathas and Afghans

186. The Quit India Movement was launched in
A. 1930
B. 1940
C. 1942
D. 1946

187. The Partition of Bengal in 1905 was done by
A. Lord Curzon
B. Lord Wellesley
C. Hastings
D. Ripon

188. Which of the following is *not* a Himalayan river?
A. Saryu
B. Alakananda
C. Mandakini
D. Narmada

189. Which is known as the home of the Asiatic lions?
A. Gir National Park
B. Dudhwa National Park
C. Kanha National Park
D. Corbett National Park

190. One of the states through which the Tropic of Cancer passes is
A. Jammu and Kashmir
B. Bihar
C. Himachal Pradesh
D. Jharkhand

191. Which river forms its delta in Orissa?
A. Krishna
B. Mahanadi
C. Godavari
D. Kaveri

192. Which state is the leading producer of red chillies?
A. Punjab
B. Karnataka
C. West Bengal
D. Andhra Pradesh

193. What is Raniganj famous for?
A. Iron ore
B. Coal
C. Manganese
D. Mica

194. The ideals of Liberty, Equality and Fraternity enshrined in the Preamble of the Constitution of India were adopted under inspiration from
A. The Russian Revolution
B. The American Declaration of Independence
C. The U.N. Charter
D. The French Revolution

195. The President of India is
A. the Head of the State
B. the Head of the Government
C. the Head of the Government as well as the State
D. None of the above

196. The Vice President of India is
A. directly elected by the people
B. elected by the same electoral college which elects the President
C. elected by the members of Lok Sabha and Rajya Sabha at a joint meeting
D. elected by the members of Rajya Sabha alone

197. Which one of the following did *not* occupy the office of the Prime Minister?
A. Jagjivan Ram
B. Morarji Desai
C. Chandra Shekhar
D. Both (A) and (C)

198. The Official Language of India is
A. English
B. Hindi
C. Tamil
D. Urdu

199. The 42nd Amendment to the Constitution
A. introduced Fundamental Duties for the first time
B. made the Directive Principles justiciable
C. made elementary education as a Fundamental Right
D. did none of the above

200. Who was the first Speaker of the Lok Sabha?
A. Hukum Singh
B. G.S. Dhillon
C. Ananthaswayanam Ayengar
D. G.V. Mavalankar

ANSWERS

1	2	3	4	5	6	7	8	9	10
B	B	A	B	D	B	C	A	A	C

11	12	13	14	15	16	17	18	19	20
B	B	C	A	A	B	C	D	D	C

21	22	23	24	25	26	27	28	29	30
B	A	C	D	A	D	C	A	A	A

31	32	33	34	35	36	37	38	39	40
B	B	C	B	B	D	B	C	C	B

41	42	43	44	45	46	47	48	49	50
C	C	C	C	B	A	A	A	D	C

51	52	53	54	55	56	57	58	59	60
B	A	D	A	D	D	D	A	D	A

61	62	63	64	65	66	67	68	69	70
A	C	A	A	D	D	C	D	D	B

71	72	73	74	75	76	77	78	79	80
B	A	B	C	C	B	B	C	D	A

81	82	83	84	85	86	87	88	89	90
B	C	C	B	A	A	D	C	D	C

91	92	93	94	95	96	97	98	99	100
D	C	C	C	A	D	C	D	B	A

101	102	103	104	105	106	107	108	109	110
D	C	C	D	C	C	C	A	B	C

111	112	113	114	115	116	117	118	119	120
C	A	C	A	A	C	D	B	D	A

121	122	123	124	125	126	127	128	129	130
A	A	A	B	D	C	B	B	D	A

131	132	133	134	135	136	137	138	139	140
A	A	A	B	D	C	B	B	D	A

141	142	143	144	145	146	147	148	149	150
C	C	B	B	C	D	A	A	B	B

151	152	153	154	155	156	157	158	159	160
A	A	C	B	A	A	A	C	B	A

161	162	163	164	165	166	167	168	169	170
B	C	B	C	B	A	A	B	A	A

171	172	173	174	175	176	177	178	179	180
A	B	B	C	B	D	B	A	C	C

181	182	183	184	185	186	187	188	189	190
B	C	D	D	D	C	A	D	A	D

191	192	193	194	195	196	197	198	199	200
B	D	B	D	C	C	A	B	A	D